FEARLESS MEN

*Conquer the Struggles, Insecurities, and Pressures
Threatening Your Soul*

BY DAVE NOVAK

ISBN: 979-8-218-45613-9 (E-book)
ISBN: 979-8-218-45612-2 (Paperback)

Dave Novak Ministries
5050 Laguna Blvd. Unit 112 #770
Elk Grove, California

Email: dave@davenovakministries.com

Website: Davenovakministrties.com

Book Cover design @sam_designs1. Edited by @Marc_Writer

Italics or bold lettering are used to indicate emphasis, narration, or thoughts of the author.

Scripture

DEDICATION

To my son, Titus.

This book is written as a gift for you. Fearlessly serve God with all your life, for the rest of your life. I'm proud to be your dad and I love you.

Love, Dad.

Contents

THANK YOUS

Thank you to the following men who have impacted my life for decades and helped me become the best version of myself. Though I've only shared these men, there are many more faithful friends who have helped mold me into the man I am today. We have shared personal moments together; you know who you are. I'm grateful for our friendship.

Adam Sikorksi – thank you for empowering and inspiring me in my late twenties to be a confident man with flaws, insecurities, struggles, while unashamedly exercising my gifts and talents. This book would not have happened without you.

Pastor Coco Perez – thank you for modeling what a spiritual father is, and demonstrating commitment to family first.

Andrew Huson and Hector Gutierrez – thank you for your lifelong friendships, strengthening and supporting me in key seasons. You are both definitions of what it means to "stick closer than a brother".

Pastor Bret Allen – thank you for introducing me to leadership and inspiring me to develop my own.

FEAR

An intense emotion in response to a danger or threat.

"FEAR NOT"

– Jesus

WHY FEARLESS MEN?

I was seated with seven guys at our church's conference table, fighting back tears as I felt myself beginning to cry. I dropped my head as the tears finally started streaming down my cheeks and I covered my mouth as my chin began to quiver. Then I looked up at the men, and I realized we were all emotional. I was about to break down. Yeah, I'm a little bit of a softy.

It was a Saturday morning meeting I had planned for a group of guys in our church. The Lord had given me a vision for a small, invitation only group to start growing as Christian men. The group was to have somewhat of a boot camp feel. The men who gathered with me weren't "top level" religious men in our church. I searched for men I felt wanted to grow, had a hunger for God, but didn't know how to get what they desired to become…an authentic Christian.

These guys were entering into a high-level journey which I believed would bring high-level results. Each time I individually proposed this opportunity to each man, they commonly responded with, "I need that, I want that". I made it very clear this was going to cause potential inconveniences with their personal lives. I wouldn't allow the married guys to commit without their wives agreeing to what would be required. I told each of them this would come with non-negotiables. They would have to be extremely committed (on time, can't miss bi-weekly Saturdays for nine months, also attend and serve every Sunday), extremely transparent (reveal past pain and current struggles), extremely accountable (complete every assignment and explain why if you didn't), and keep extreme confidence (no other men knew about this group and not one word

1

could be mentioned outside of our meetings). I had never heard of anything like this, so I communicated we'd be learning as I carefully led.

The goal was simple; be a godly man in every area of their lives, inside and out. Their ambition must be to honor God with their lives; learning from what He teaches, living in His ways, and being loyal to His truth. They should carry themselves as godly men in the difficulties and struggles of life. I stressed each time they walk into any room the climate should be impacted. Understanding their standard as a godly man should impact their families, coworkers, classmates, buddies, and more.

2 Peter 1:3 (NLT) states, *"His divine power has given us everything we need for a godly life"*. The English word "godly" in this scripture comes from the Greek word *eusebiea,* meaning inner reverence, spiritual maturity, and religious virtues. I communicated to these men my "pastor hat" would come off occasionally in these meetings and I would put on a "coach's hat"; pushing them to become this very definition and reflect it outwardly. I believed in them, and they had in trust me.

Back to the heavy, emotional meeting on that Saturday.

I was about to break down as a middle-aged man was sharing about private, hidden experiences in his childhood, and he explained he had never shared these with anyone before, not even his wife. He was traumatized by the sexual abuse he endured by a family friend over a long period. He had been living in shame, silently carrying the scars all his life, and having a low self-esteem. Full of tears most of the time he talked, he would briefly stop when he was close to weeping.

When this brave man concluded, I'll never forget the comment a younger man made sitting across from him. He somberly and plainly said, "I thought I was the only one". I couldn't hold it in any longer as I began to weep. This grieved my soul in a way I hadn't felt with men in a church setting. Men living their lives in silent pain, blocking out memories, and lacking confidence to overcome areas of defeat. Convinced they are alone.

FULL OF MESSY CHURCHES

It was then I realized we have churches filled with men, discouraged, and intimidated by life history and unable conquer current struggles, sitting in the chair next to us each Sunday. They aren't experiencing the abundant, free life Jesus promised. They're merely going through virtuous and religious motions.

How has this happened?

It's not intentional I just believe in church circles we're uncomfortable getting into "messes" and afraid religious rules will be violated. So, men in particular fear being judged, and they won't share anything. What if churches welcomed men to share their mess, without anyone having a "to-do" list ready for them so they fit into our controlling, religious molds? We need to normalize messes to talk unashamedly.

Since church communities are insecure about venturing into these issues, we simply preach at men hoping they will do what we tell them. I've been to many men's conferences, retreats, and events where we do this. Even I've done it at times as a lead pastor. We borderline chastise them for not doing their jobs. We've been teaching men what to do all the while long we have not helped men heal and break free from struggles. Since the church isn't bold enough to go in the messy places of a man's soul, neither are men. We don't have fearless men, but fragile men.

Its time churches are ok with habits, addictions, or attitudes men aren't proud of and allow men to fearlessly process and grow in areas they've been stuck. This book is for men who have anger issues, abuse substances, have porn addictions, gay men, depressed men, isolated men, Christian or non-Christian, have secret sins, molested men, alcoholic men, abusive men, racist men, murderers, bi-sexual men, or those identifying as transexual or transgender (biologically male). I want you to know if you are in any of these areas, you're not alone. Even if you've been a Christian for 30 years, you're not there yet. See, it's ok not to be ok, but it's not ok to stay that way.

As a lead pastor over 15 years, and more than 25 in full-time ministry, I've watched men in churches struggle and even give up on following Christ. This is a problem we can no longer overlook or just apply band-aids. As I have sat down with hundreds in one-on-one or in group settings, who were dissatisfied or defeated, I gave them tools and encouragement to be the man *they* grew to respect and love.

In this book I'm going to take you on that same journey to discover what you're created for, how to make changes where you feel necessary, and live authentic and wholeheartedly for Christ. This decision can't be put off another day; it's an opportunity to become a greater man without limitations. I promise as you give your time to read though every chapter, you will find yourself more confident and happier than you are today. So do it for you, right now.

A FEARLESS MAN

What a fearless man consists of is dropping the "tough guy" guard on the outside that hides the confused, damaged, and insecure issues on the inside. It's simply self-sabotage. Self-sabotage means to act in a way which undermines personal progress by managing weakness stemming from fear. It's fear of being exposed, ridiculed, looked down on, and ostracized. Or even worse, considered to be less of a man. We're so fatigued presenting the "play the man" image.

To become a Fearless Man requires courage to *conquer the struggles, insecurities, and pressures threatening your masculinity*. Fearlessness and courage can be defined as "the willingness to let go of the familiar". Too many guys do not have the courage to release the familiar coping mechanisms they have been addicted to for the purpose of being perceived as a man in the eyes of others. The fearless become bold, going into the dark, hidden places of the soul to find transformation. Few men in our generation, inside and outside of the church, do this. You don't have to live the rest of your life trying to maintain your cover.

STRAIGHT UP

I made the decision before sitting down to write, I would be transparent and direct, it's partially due to who I am. I'm not proud of many things I have done in my life; you'll read some in the upcoming pages. Whether they be sexually, relationally, fathering, career, spiritually, or in married life. I am uncomfortably honest because, why would you be if I'm not? Presenting partial openness would be false transparency and shallow authenticity. These do not reflect fearless, courageous men, but they lean more toward cowardice.

I'm not going to boast of personal victories, but rather reveal areas I fight to gain ground and witness God's power. Pastor and author Craig Groeschel says, "We impress with our strengths, but we connect in our weakness." We're in this together so I promise to be truthful about areas I'm growing and developing as a man. I can tell you this, I want to become great and better in the eyes of God without a sense of earning his acceptance. I will do anything, as hard and as intimidating it may be, to honor God with my life. It's all up to me. I aspire to possess a spirit in this book as the Apostle Paul expressed, *"My eager desire and hope being…I may do honor to Christ in my own person by fearless courage. Whether that means life or death, no matter!"* (Philippians 1:20 Moffat). Living godly will be my life pursuit until the day I die. Period.

This book isn't based on the heroic feats of popular men in the Bible, but rather learning from their downfalls and struggles, which we can identify with most. It's not packed with "How-to's", or steps to have spiritual habits and disciplines. I do believe as you read through each chapter you will find yourself possessing an increased craving to have regular practices.

Each chapter has true life stories of men whose names I have changed to protect their privacy. These are men I have encountered in one way or another over decades of pastoral ministry. I intentionally include some instances which are taboo in church and borderline graphic, not to sensationalize but relate to struggles many men face.

Following each chapter there will be Courage Questions. I encourage you to take a few moments to process each of them and write down your answer to them. I believe this will help you conquer areas that have sabotaged the greatness in your manhood.

My goal is for a new generation of fearless men to arise…without flinching. The time is short. Tomorrow is not promised. Your friends, family, and coworkers need you to be fearless.

If you will fearlessly face what's lurking inside, you can fearlessly face what's happening on the outside.

Let's become Fearless Men together.

COURAGE QUESTIONS

1. What has been an overarching fear or disappointment in your life you struggle to conquer? Why?

2. What are you hoping to discover and overcome by reading this book?

THE STRUGGLES NOBODY SEES

For about three weeks I was wrestling with a question I felt compelled to ask my wife. It was one in which I knew the answer and I feared the answer at the same time. I would decide to ask her on several occasions, then chicken out and put it off.

As I was driving on the freeway with her in the passenger seat one day, I just decided to do it. I asked her, "Are you happy in our marriage?" We weren't headed for divorce; I just knew things weren't good and we were more like roommates who tolerated each other rather than demonstrating love. Even though we were leading a church, there was tension at home.

Why did I feel I needed to ask the question? One reason was when I was in my teens in a time of dumb adolescent behavior someone close to me carelessly stated, "You'll never stay married in the future. You will end up divorced." Those words never left me and here I was imagining the worst in my marriage. I was afraid that would come true, though we were far from it. More than failing in marriage, I didn't want to hurt my wife or make her life miserable. It was a struggle I wrestled with. I wasn't going let it happen, so I boldly chose to get the cold hard truth.

"No" was the short response to my question. It was painful yet sobering to hear. I said "ok" as we rode in silence to our destination. I inwardly concluded I had work to do. I refused to put it on her. I chose not to spout off with, "Well if you would only _____" or "You're not doing your part". I owned the responsibility as the man in our home. I didn't make efforts to improve to kiss up to my wife but to navigate us into a healthier home and marriage; one we both enjoyed.

God didn't ordain my wife to lead, he appointed me. I began establishing new practices for myself. I believed how she felt reflected my patterns. Without telling her I was going to form new habits; I just implemented them. I would come into the house with a better attitude. I would practice being a servant rather than her catering to me. My tone changed to a softer one when I spoke. I met with a mentor and a counselor to help me grow and change my behavior. It was heavy lifting for me but well worth it. As things improved, I scheduled date nights and getaways without the kids.

Nobody, not friends, my kids, people in our church knew the things I was doing, nor did they understand what I was up to. My inward struggle was threatening me, but I wouldn't allow it to control me. If I hadn't faced the fear, I would spend a life compensating for my weaknesses and faults. It could have sabotaged my relationship with my wife because I was afraid to take responsibility and do the work.

SABOTAGED MANHOOD

Our society gives automatic promotion into manhood at the age of 18. People in places of influence define what a man should be while criticizing and condemning men at the same time. As I found on my journey, like most, I had to live assuming I'd discover the day I'd stop referring myself as just a "guy" and be able to have self-confidence to say, "I'm a man".

I'm not a fan of the term, "Real Man". I believe you're either a man, or just male. A male animal or human is only identified by his genitals with nothing else mattering. If we don't define what a man is, it's left to anybody create to their own ideals, preferences, and conclusions which lead to toxic masculinity.

A couple years prior to Covid-19 breaking out, a man emerged to prominence in multiple media outlets and became a sensation. He became one of the top worldwide figures through social media platforms and younger generations were drawn to hear what he would communicate regarding manhood. He has been interviewed by many well-known news reporters and columnists due to his grandiose persona. I'll refer to him as Adam, mainly to not give him anymore airtime and influence.

Adam is an individual of great bravado and strong stature with millions of followers on Instagram, Tik Tok, YouTube, and Facebook. He is a self-made millionaire in the hundreds, owning private jets and yachts, and he is a four-time world kickboxing champion. It has been reported he has a very high IQ, making him greatly successful in all his ventures. He isn't shy about highlighting his achievements and literally declaring he has no weaknesses nor any negativity within. His confidence is through the roof, intimidating, and commands people to acquiesce to his narratives…because he doesn't seem to fail in anything.

Adam is domineering, airing his opinions and views, literally stating he is "God's force for good". Some of his perspectives are traditional, partially noble, and mostly controversial. He condemns lazy men and those who view pornography. He mocks men who deal with depression. Adam declares men should take care of their children and women; though he gives himself freedom to have multiple relationships. He speaks out against government corruption, while minimizing any accusations of him having it as well. He preaches male supremacy and is a self-proclaimed misogynist, not trusting women and openly sexist. Not only men but numerous ladies give him their ears. He believes he is a role model for young men who are powerless and unsure of themselves, challenging them to be like him. His identity and sense of purpose are seemingly irresistible to men lacking direction.

Adam imposes his "pure" masculinity and his inability to be defeated by anything or anyone. He refuses to acknowledge the possibility of failure. Millions of young men don't know how to possess confident masculinity so they're listening to Adam because it is so attractive and appears to be true.

But there is a disguised struggle nobody sees in Adam which he refuses to accept exists.

In a recorded two-hour conversation with a psychologist, Adam revealed many deep-rooted, emotional issues. As he uncovered them, he didn't even appear to know what was coming out of his mouth. In the interview Adam was asked questions about times when he had experienced discouragement and negativity, which he vehemently dismissed ever having. When asked to share any insecurities or weaknesses he may have, he arrogantly denied them. As the psychologist pressed him asking how he responds when hurt, Adam was silent. He nervously explained he hadn't been asked that before. He was squirming in his seat. He literally could not respond. At one point the psychologist asked – knowing the answer – about how his dad treated him. Adam stammered trying to give an answer, but changed the subject.

Adam's dad was a large, strong, brilliant, and demanding father who expected only success and perfection from Adam. Fear and defeat were unacceptable. He would intentionally put Adam at a merciless disadvantage to make things hard for Adam to succeed. Adam once stated when he was a toddler his dad used to knock him down. Forcefully pushing him to the ground repeatedly for years. He learned to backpedal quickly, which only made his dad push him harder. His dad showed him no love as he grew up. So, Adam developed a massive chip on his shoulder.

Adam's dad passed away more than a decade ago and he continues to strive for success, be perfect, fight to win, lord over others, and never fail, to please his dad. Along with this he elevates, and condemns, himself above men and women to boost confidence.

Adam is hiding internal struggles and tension nobody sees…but it is sabotaging a truly content and fulfilling life emotionally and relationally. He has weaknesses he is afraid to address and heal. He is controlled in areas he cannot confront; fearful he can't win. I believe at the core, he really is a good man who believes in good values, but he's a broken man in need of healing.

Fearless men are willing to face what threatens their manhood without compensating with a façade.

SHEDDING LIGHT ON THE STRUGGLE

When we're hiding struggles, we can't admit we are incapable, at fault, powerless, or hurt because we fear being labeled as weak. We are sabotaging the opportunity to gain strength in areas of weakness. We are afraid and spend time trying to prove manhood. We hide in caves, shut down, stay distant, fight addictions, and lean towards anything that can help avoid conquering the distress in our souls. We compensate for real shortcomings with false strength. We're not strong, we're hiding.

We are wrestling with stored up issues, not knowing how to address them, with the threat of losing. We might experience tension in forms of animosity, anxiety, inadequacy, perceived incompetence, approval, wounds, rejection and more. These are sabotaging our ethics, performance, spirituality, relationships, careers and more. We don't know what to do so we "man up", become a "real man", or play the "tough guy".

What if you dared to bring the internal struggle to light and chose to shamelessly conquer it? That is fearless.

Each of us have fears and weaknesses we wish were non-existent. So, we might believe if they're unseen we'll be ok. But it's tension we find ourselves trying to manage at times. When truthfully, our weaknesses and struggles will eventually show themselves and influence areas in our lives.

A fearless man makes the bold and brave decision to defeat the hidden turmoil, not allowing it to have power any longer.

THE MYSTERIOUS STRUGGLE

There's a mighty man in the Bible who had an incredibly fearless moment. We're not sure why he did what he did, but there was certainly something internal that compelled him.

Benaiah, son of Jehoiada, was a valiant fighter from Kabzeel, who performed great exploits. He struck down two of Moab's best

13

men. _He also went down into a pit on a snowy day and killed a lion_. And he struck down a huge Egyptian. Although the Egyptian had a spear in his hand, Benaiah went against him with a club. He snatched the spear from the Egyptian's hand and killed him with his own spear. Such were the exploits of Benaiah, son of Jehoiada; he too was as famous as the three mighty men. He was held in greater honor than any of the Thirty, but he was not included among the Three. And David put him in charge of his bodyguard. 2 Samuel 23:20-23.

The underlined words are the phrases I want to focus on. What would motivate a man to chase a lion and kill it, in a pit, on a snowy day? Sure, we understand defeating the warriors mentioned who were the opposition, but why the lion? There's absolutely no reason to kill a lion on the run. What a sight to see as an onlooker.

Is it possible there was internal conflict Benaiah was wrestling with? What was the tension driving him?

He didn't have to kill the lion to prove anything…or did he?

In the beginning of the passages above it describes Benaiah as brave and mighty. He was better than the top 30 warriors in the army, then five words are used which might have been the tipping point for Benaiah's struggle. When it came to David's top three mighty men, the words _"but he was not included"_ described Benaiah's status. He was greater than most and leader over bodyguards, but not good enough or elite like the three.

Could it be this is what drove Benaiah to kill the lion? Was this the tension he suffered from? Did he feel a need to prove himself worthy? It would be understandable if he was injured by his placement. Why couldn't there be four if he was _"just as famous as the three"_? Did he feel left out, rejected, or not valued? Maybe not good or strong enough and perceived as incompetent? He could have developed self-doubt and inadequacy, questioning his identity.

What a tough place to exist while being strong enough to hold back emotions or wuss out. I've seen these issues arise in men, and even myself. Spending our lives trying to measure up and be a true man.

We don't specifically know what the threat and struggle was residing in this great man. But we do see the actions revealing his posture to defeat the internal conflict. Three things in Benaiah stand out to me that can serve as tips we can gather from this courageous encounter with the lion. They reflect the spirit of a fearless man. These characteristics will be helpful to possess reading the rest of this book as we dare to conquer what's sabotage our present and future.

A FEARLESS MAN WILL ACKNOWLEDGE HIS STRUGGLES

Benaiah *"went down into a pit"* where he was in the dark, alone, vulnerable, outweighed, cornered, and only he knew the struggle. He would find out what his deficiencies and liabilities were, which denial or pretending wouldn't be helpful. It was time to get real. If he was going to come out of the pit alive, he had to be honest with himself and fight through his weakness.

Your bravest move is when you will be honest about your struggle to grow and overcome it.

What's a stronghold or insecurity deep down you avoid? What behavior do you hate about yourself? Where are you suffering? What's the unwanted craving? What hinders your relationship with God? What's mastering you? What shortcomings, weaknesses, things you're not proud of, secrets, or sin is threatening you? It's time to be honest and own it.

Secure and confident men are willing to admit they need to make changes. Get this – insecure men can only talk about their strengths and accomplishments. Every man has a struggle within. Remember you're not alone. Evaluate where you lack and start winning the fight!

A FEARLESS MAN WILL SEIZE HIS STRUGGLES

The scripture doesn't mention Benaiah waiting for better weather conditions or the sun to shine because it would be more favorable for victory. It states he accomplished this *"on a snowy day"*. It was freezing, his hands were probably numb, and more than likely the rocks were slippery. The conditions did not deter him. He decided, it dies today.

What conditions are you waiting for? Are you making excuses blaming other people or waiting for them to take responsibility? Would you rather appear tough while you're angry and defensive? Wouldn't it be better to live the rest of your life as a healed and confident man instead of a broken and defeated man?

The New Living Translation of the Bible reads *"he chased a lion"*. Benaiah didn't delay, make excuses, minimize it, procrastinate, or try to manage it. How long do you want to live with issues that sabotage areas of your life? Go after *your* lion! Nobody can decide to kill the struggle within but you.

A FEARLESS MAN WILL DEFEAT HIS STRUGGLES

What a reputation to have, *"he killed a lion"*. I'd love to be described that way, but truth be told I'd more likely dance, run zigzag, hide, and more to stay alive if a lion was on the loose. Benaiah decided this lion was going to die once and for all. He wasn't going to live looking over his shoulder wondering when it would show up and cause a disturbance again. He saw the sharp teeth, felt the powerful roar, then looked into the eyes of the lion and started the fight. Once he started the fight, there was no turning back.

Sadly, too often we have struggles we tolerate and try to manage instead of taking a stand and defeating them. We live ignoring, avoiding, "trying", and dancing around the weaknesses and conflicts instead of intentionally saying I'm not going to live this way anymore. When it comes to your struggle, you have to kill it, or it will continue to kill you.

Only one of them was coming out of that pit alive. They fought to the death, and we don't know how long. But Benaiah was the one celebrating victory. Today let's decide to defeat whatever struggle you may identify with in this book and never accept anything but victory again. Do not quit until you have conquered the struggles you recognize have been sabotaging your life.

Throughout this book carry this mentality to acknowledge, seize, and defeat the struggle that resonates within you. *"No weapon formed against you will prosper"* unless you give in to it.

As I have reflected on making corrections to have a better marriage, I recognized these three perspectives were at work in me. It wasn't easy to look inside myself and be honest about my shortcomings, faults, and attitudes. But if I wanted things to improve, I had to personally choose to address them and be real with myself, no longer pretending everything was ok. I didn't want to make things look ok on the outside layers, but trouble was present as I avoided it because it was too hard. I have made a commitment to confront every struggle head on instead so I can live a future healthy and confident as a fearless man. Because I took action, my wife and I developed a greater bond and unity together. I worked hard while nobody knew or cared to know.

In the upcoming pages things are going to get "real". Let's conquer these areas that sabotage…and live fearless.

COURAGE QUESTIONS

1. What is one struggle or secret you have carried from childhood? Where did it come from?

2. As you have grown into a man, what is an area you have wrestled with and never been able to master? Why?

3. Are you ready to work on areas of weakness, shame, or failure no matter what it takes? Explain why.

EXPOSED HE-MOTIONS
VULNERABILITY

– The Elijah Struggle –

"Just kill yourself".

I'm almost embarrassed to admit that phrase was playing out in my mind. Those were the words I kept hearing in a Sunday morning service minutes before I was supposed to preach. "Just take your life", "everyone will understand", "no one will miss you or blame you for doing it". Strong statements I'd never had in my mind. I'm a very mind over matter, make it happen kind of guy...until this dark day snuck up on me.

The church we started had been growing and was meeting on Sundays in different schools for six years. It was now a season we felt we should acquire a space to lease for our church to finally a permanent location. This was an exciting new phase I had been looking forward to and, as we were demolishing and remodeling the inside a facility, I was full of vision. This project took several months to complete but two thirds of the way through we hit some walls. We were running out of money, income from the church had decreased, building plans with the city were getting held up, and new rent was due while we were still renting schools. We couldn't continue and we couldn't retreat. Over the weeks of this dilemma my stress and discouragement were getting the best of me. It was a stalemate.

Earlier that week I remember walking through the unfinished, hoped-to-be sanctuary, that was silent with supplies and materials stacked with no work happening. I was so upset, helpless, and even embarrassed because, I'm the leader so it's my fault. I'm supposed to be the man with the answers. In prayer that day as I was walking, I started to break down. It was a mixture of frustration, anger, desperation, and fear. So, I did what most men would do, I muscled through and quit my snivelin'.

That next Sunday I was in the worship singing portion of our service and started thinking, "I don't want to be here, I don't want to talk, or preach". That's a really bad plan for a guy whose main "workday" is Sunday where he has to do those very things. Then I heard those cruel statements, "just kill yourself", in a variety of styles. I preached and talked then went home. From 10am that morning until the following morning those phrases kept haunting me. It was odd because I wasn't saying them to myself, I was hearing them. I knew if I allowed this voice to keep speaking to me all alone, something dangerous could happen. Suicide was never in my past thoughts or a struggle for me, but that day a foul spirit was harassing me.

I did something I knew had to happen. I had learned over the years to never try to fight big battles on your own. *Ecclesiastes 4:10-11 reads, "Two are better than one…Pity the man who falls and has no one to help him up! If two lie down together, they will keep warm. But how can one keep warm alone?"* I had established dear friends which would be to my benefit in unplanned moments like these. I decided I needed in the biggest way to bring other close friends into my vulnerable state. I told my wife what was happening, and then called two of my closest friends and talked with them separately as they generously gave me their time to hear me out. I knew they would drop what they were doing. I let loose unfiltered telling them what was happening, how I was feeling, where I was trying to act like I had it all together. I was being vulnerable without holding anything back. I dread to think what might have happened if I didn't have honest, human relationships to lean on and have something dangerous happen, while I tried to fight through on my own. They were lifesavers.

VULNERABILITY IS FOR THE WEAK

When us guys are encouraged to be vulnerable, it can be an intimidating and a very uncomfortable task. Mostly because we have an inaccurate view of vulnerability being in a position for others to attack, criticize, damage, or hurt you. Why would anyone want to put themselves in that situation? We commonly see vulnerability as a weakness…and if you're a dude, it's stupid.

Let's be honest, ladies cry together, go to the restroom together, tell each other they're cute. With us, we don't invite each other to the restroom, we DO NOT look at each other in the eyes while in there, we keep our eyes facing the wall as we're standing at a urinal we picked furthest from any other guy. In addition, I've never told a friend he looked nice, cute, was good looking or handsome when he's looking his best. The closest we get to any compliment is, "Hey man, where'd you get that shirt?"

I remember when my son Titus played tackle football on a team for seven-year-old boys. It's etched in my mind when another boy got his "bell rung" and he was beginning to cry, and was maybe a little scared too. He went over to his dad and his dad forcefully and uncaringly said, "Quit crying, boy! Wipe your tears!" I felt bad for the kid who needed some concern and reassurance rather than being scolded for crying. I think the father was probably a victim of the same treatment at some point and even in that moment intimidated by what may appear being a "soft" man or having a "soft" son.

Many, as boys, are directly or indirectly instructed not to cry, because "only sissies cry". Hold it back in front of people and, then when alone, you can let it out. Through this what we're really saying is, don't be vulnerable. Don't let people see you weak. Men aren't soft.

We end up avoiding vulnerability by appearing strong, only talking about strengths, hide shortcomings, keep people emotionally distant, don't confess sin, won't ask for help, deny fears, and cover up mistakes. Boy, what a man!

When we set up walls to protect, they actually isolate.

Hear me friend, it takes an incredibly confident and fearless man to be vulnerable. Bold and secure men are willing to be vulnerable because they understand it improves their lives. If you are willing, you will benefit from this form of honesty and find yourself more confident.

According to James Madison University Counseling Center, "vulnerability is the core of emotions and feelings. If we prevent ourselves from being vulnerable, we foreclose on experiencing our emotions. Our attempts to prevent shame, embarrassment, and sadness also prevent us from experiencing love, belonging, joy, and empathy". In her book *Daring Greatly*, Dr Brene Brown further explains, "Vulnerability is the birthplace of love, belonging, joy, courage, empathy, and creativity." When we dare to be vulnerable, we empower ourselves to have a better quality of life.

Vulnerability is an asset we've been cheated of if we have never practiced it. So why don't we do it? Because it threatens to take away our "man card" and freaks us out! We have a hard time being vulnerable because that means we must open up about difficult areas like intimacy with our wife outside of sex, exposing weaknesses, sharing dreams, what we suck at, talking about our failures and what we're ashamed of, dark feelings we have, and more. None of us are alone in these. These reflect the "He-motions" of men, trying to discover what we're allowed to feel as healthy and strong.

We're naturally worried about what will people think, and we don't want to appear stupid or weak. Vulnerability is especially hard when you've only been surrounded by toxic, unhealthy, or untrustworthy people most of your life.

There are statements most men are fearful of confessing as the perception these are weakness. Bold and secure men have a growing confidence to say things like: "I love you", "I don't know", "I'm afraid of…", "I was wrong", "I need help", "I'm alone", or "I'm failing". They are also shamelessly willing to shed tears, give physical affection when it is uncomfortable, and forgive instead of getting revenge of those who maliciously attacked them. I admire men who openly express these. They're fearless.

VICTORIOUSLY VULNERABLE

There was a man, I'll call Javier, I invited to join the men's group I described in the beginning of the book. Being part of this group came with high expectations, which included being totally transparent in every area of your life. I believed Javier was a perfect addition. He would have some much-needed breakthroughs in areas I knew about, and I believe he desired to have them.

For most of his life he was attracted to men and had numerous homosexual encounters. This was an unwanted attraction he hated and, whenever he would talk with me about it, he would cry. He loved the Lord and attended church for years, but he always felt God tolerated him and Javier wasn't going to be allowed to live a full abundant life because of the lifestyle he knew was sinful in God's eyes. He would keep this silent and never mention it to anyone due to fear of rejection or abandonment.

When I asked him to join the group he answered yes, after praying, under one condition. He wanted me to promise he wouldn't have to share about his big secret. I told him I must uphold the structure of the group and he wouldn't be the only one sharing dark or shameful secrets. So, I said, you'll end up having to share. But I did make one promise to him, "you'll be glad you shared it". He nervously committed to the group.

The day came when Javier shared his unwanted attraction. Keeping his eyes on the table, he talked about it, from the pornography problem it included to how he ended up having homosexual experiences. In that moment all of us hurt for his frustration and the pain he cried with. We were broken in the room that day. Each guy shared how they believed he was brave and would stand with him. I was so proud of Javier. That day he was a Fearless Man I respected. It ended up being one of the best moments of his life.

If Javier had never opened up and became vulnerable, he wouldn't have discovered his courage, received praise for sharing, enjoyed comfort, nor had a greater embrace for his church community. We all hugged him that day with strong brotherly love from the Lord.

No matter how great, successful, or Christian you become, you will always experience weak points in your life when vulnerability is the way through.

NOT VULNERABLE

Elijah was a successful minister in the Old Testament. He was a prophet God used to perform miracles and be His voice to lead people. Elijah was normal like us men today, as we'll see in this short story about him. I've found encouragement in Elijah's story because I can personally relate to how he felt.

This passage follows a powerful, spiritual contest Elijah had with 850 prophets of two pagan gods against his Most High God. The goal was simple, yet almost impossible. The way they would find out who served the true god is when they took turns praying. The 850 were to pray first and Elijah second, and the real god would answer from heaven with fire, burning an altar with a bull, wood, on stones. When the 850 prophets prayed, nothing happened but after Elijah prayed, his God answered with a consuming fire. Then because the 850 were now found as false prophets, according to Moses' law, they had to be executed, so Elijah carried that out. This did not go over well with the king's evil wife, Jezebel. Those prophets were part of her worship and she recruited them. Here's what followed this event.

> *Ahab reported to Jezebel everything that Elijah had done, including the massacre of the prophets. Jezebel immediately sent a messenger to Elijah with her threat: "The gods will get*

*you for this and I'll get even with you! By this time tomorrow
you'll be as dead as any one of those prophets." When Elijah
saw how things were, he ran for dear life to Beer-sheba, far in
the south of Judah. He left his servant there and then went on
into the desert another day's journey. He came to a lone broom
bush and collapsed in its shade, wanting in the worst way to
be done with it all—to just die: "Enough of this, GOD! Take my
life—I'm ready to join my ancestors in the grave!" Exhausted, he
fell asleep under the lone broom bush. Suddenly an angel shook
him awake and said, "Get up and eat!" He looked around and, to
his surprise, right by his head were a loaf of bread baked on some
coals and a jug of water. He ate the meal and went back to sleep.
The angel of GOD came back, shook him awake again, and said,
"Get up and eat some more—you've got a long journey ahead
of you." He got up, ate and drank his fill, and set out. Nourished
by that meal, he walked 40 days and nights, all the way to the
mountain of God, to Horeb. When he got there, he crawled into
a cave and went to sleep. Then the word of GOD came to him:
"So Elijah, what are you doing here?" "I've been working my
heart out for the GOD-of-the-Angel-Armies," said Elijah. "The
people of Israel have abandoned your covenant, destroyed the
places of worship, and murdered your prophets. I'm the only one
left, and now they're trying to kill me." (2 Kings 19:1-10 NLT)*

How incredible is this story? This powerful prophet goes into
depression to the point of suicide...after a miraculous act of God.
See, he was unbelievably fragile just as we can be.

I'm convinced a crucial, first mistake Elijah made occurred when *"he
left his servant there and went on"*. The only other man, one who was with
him constantly, he now abandoned to be alone in his sad and low state.
He could have kept him with him and took a few gritty moments to be
vulnerable to make it through. Sure, he had an angel arrive and assist
him, and we could too, but let's not take on another cowardly cover up

by getting overly spiritual and say, "I only need God". When God created man, he was clear it wasn't good for man to be alone, because we all need healthy and dependable relationships. We see, here with Elijah, what the results can be if we choose to be alone like him.

H.A.L.T.

H.A.L.T. is an acrostic which will warn you of the importance of vulnerable relationships, when you begin to feel what it describes. We don't start waving the white flag after we have been beat up, rather we look for yellow (warning) flags for us to stop and evaluate our condition. We see these yellow flags in the scriptures. These are some practical signs we're not headed for a good place and it's time to push pause.

Hungry
Elijah was noticeably starving. When starvation occurs in our bodies, our metabolism slows, our body can't regulate temperature, the immune system weakens, and the heart and lungs can shrink. Your body is beginning to break down and won't last. Hunger is a warning that it's time to eat and restore health.

Angry
Elijah blurts out in irritation and frustration; *"Enough of this God"*, and *"I've been working my heart out"*. It's in a moment he has become emotional. He's hurt. Hurt is a cousin to anger; guys hesitate to identify hurt because that can be viewed as soft. His hurt could have easily come from nobody caring or helping him, he was unappreciated, or he was just angry at God for his current obstacle. Anger is a warning.

Lonely
Elijah went away to a *"lone broom bush and collapsed"*. He found himself all alone, no one to catch him when he was falling, probably went deeper in grief, and ended up in that state because he played the tough guy on his own. This can make us become prideful when we don't want to appear

weak and incapable of handling problems. He went from being alone to isolation. Loneliness is a warning,

Tired

Elijah was *"Exhausted"*. Weary, discouraged, and depressed people have arrived there many times where they are empty. So, they are fine with ending it and they're ready to give up.

FOUR VALUES OF VULNERABILITY

What if we had good friends, who we were be open and honest with? They would be able to spot the signs of H.A.L.T. and help us recover. The next four values are important for us to initiate to be restored, beyond the previous practical warnings, that can keep us healthy.

We should proactively seek out friendships along the way while growing these traits. If we add these emotional, practical, and spiritual reinforcements, when everything hits the fan, we're armed.

Encouragement

Elijah would become *"nourished"* from eating. You need good men to speak life into you, remind you of victories, and give you scriptural "bread" to overcome the enemy when he's attacking your spirit.

Listen

A great friend will let you be free to speak unfiltered. They are someone allowing you to dump on, share frustrations, hurts, share private things, cry, complain to, without judging. They won't be scared off when you've embarrassed yourself, done something you regret, struggle, or feel like quitting.

Present

Sometimes having someone to sit with or go on a walk with and not having to talk is important. There's a time to talk and a time to just be relaxed. They can just be around in case you need something, or to protect you from toxic behavior such as sexual, calling old friends, opening the black book, grabbing substances, self-injury, etc.

Empowerment

It is such a relief to know if I'm ever had at an extremely low point, I have friends who love and believe in me…and they will fight for me. When I'm ready to give up anything which is important (school, marriage, kids, career, etc.) they just won't allow that to happen.

Do you want the greatness wrapped in vulnerability by developing greater confidence? Be fearless by becoming the friend you need, avoid those who come across shallow or "got it together", get closer to someone headed in the right direction, and be safe for others to confide in.

As men we almost all resist small, open community with men. When small groups are provided in your church, take the bold step to practice, and become a vulnerable man acknowledging your weaknesses and struggles you wish to overcome.

How do we develop these vulnerable friendships? Be honest about where you are. You'd be amazed how much this disarms other guys and makes it easy to be vulnerable. Live out these traits and build on the healthy friendships you have with trustworthy people.

COURAGE QUESTIONS

1. Each man carries a private struggle we have a difficult time admitting. It could vary from an attitude, behavior, or action displayed at times. Are you willing to talk about it? If so, how?

2. What is an emotional wound you have kept hidden and private? What man in your life can you share it with for healing, prayer, and support? (Will you commit to contact him?)

2

AGONIZING INSECURITIES
SELF-ESTEEM

- The Jeremiah Struggle –

I'll call this man, whom I admire as a fearless man, Tyrone. He was in a position at a church as a leader who had to speak in front of people on a regular basis. It was hard for him for years and he wrestled with the thought of speaking, particularly as these were large groups. Many surveys have concluded public speaking is the number one phobia. Boy this guy was agonizing over this position and the responsibilities. Why did Tyrone have such a high dose of insecurity? Dyslexia. He struggled all through school and often tripped up in conversations and presentations all his life.

As we had coffee one day, Tyrone told me how nervous he had been for many years. He was afraid of sounding stupid and what others would think of him. Both make total sense, but those things didn't stop him. The fear is not as intense as it was before, but still arises right before it's time to step on the stage. He's come to this conclusion it's what God planned for him to do, and he will trust in Him as he steps up to the plate each time. He's got some serious stones, even when his self-esteem can be fragile.

Insecurities show themselves in ways men feel regularly. Again, we try to prevent failure or looking like an idiot. It's this struggle when who we are, or what we say, is a liability to risk, it feels uncertain, or we just simply feel incompetent. What we truly desire is a healthy self-esteem, by having a favorable opinion of oneself. Not that we want to appear cocky but being ok with what and who we are. It's a quality we admire in men who we see have "it".

Have you ever found yourself caring way too much about what others think or how you look?

ACCEPT YOUR LIMITATIONS

I'm not a hunter, mechanic, fisherman, or handyman. At times when I've evaluated my manhood, I questioned my masculine traits, and concluded, "maybe I'm less of a man". Early in our marriage, Lori and I had a very real frustration with each other. You see, her dad is a serious handyman. Nothing is too large for him to fix. He doesn't pay for people to do much work around the house or on his cars because, as a man, he believes it's his duty. So, when things needed fixing at our home or on the cars, Lori expected me to be like her dad while, on the other hand, I planned to pay for someone to take care of it. She wanted me to do things I had never been taught to do, but deep down I didn't want to screw things up. She came to a place to where she accepted me for who I am and not expect me to be her dad.

On the other hand, I struggled to accept who I am as well. Maybe I did need to be like her dad. Maybe I was failing and not trying. Maybe I was wasting money because I was a coward. I arrived at the realization I didn't need to be insecure and try to be like anyone. I needed God's help to be ok with who I am. There are a lot of other men who cannot and aren't confident in doing things I do. None of us are better or lesser of a man. I'm comfortable in my skin and I have a healthy self-esteem, which I draw from my relationship with God.

If we're not careful we end up competing and comparing ourselves to other men, which won't ever help us work through our insecurities.

Sometimes insecure guys are easy to spot because they like to talk a good game. They namedrop, exaggerate strengths, highlight accomplishments, self-promote, one-up each other, and so on. They're disguising their deficiencies, the need for attention, or lack of self-acceptance. There is no need for us to feel we must add up.

THE BEST VERSION

At times we do need to be honest about our shortcomings and be able to admit them without trying to appear like things are fine. One way we can address and overcome insecurity is becoming a teachable person who wants to grow and get better. People admire those who understand they are weak in an area – but want to do something about it.

I'm a huge San Francisco 49ers fan and I'm passionate about football. I've been a Niners fan since I was 10 years old, which is 1985. I'm writing this at a time when a new, young quarterback named Brock Purdy became a starter as a rookie with the team. I greatly admire him not only for his ability as a competitor, but as a proven man of God with integrity. He was the very last pick in the draft taking on the known name as "Mr. Irrelevant". What a title! But he has been impressive and made the Pro Bowl in his second year, starting every game. He's now recognized as "Purdy Relevant" in the NFL. The early journey was a little rocky at times, and media for some reason were waiting and wanting him to fail.

Occasionally at press conferences after questionable performances they would really go after Brock, especially noting his shortcomings. His responses weren't reflective of an insecure 23 year old man. When they addressed real problems, his response many times was, "I need to get better. I'll figure it out". Which always meant that he was going to get help from other teammates, talk to coaches, spend hours watching tape, and practice hard to overcome the challenges. And you know what? He is continually improving. This is what a confident man, with a healthy self-esteem, looks like. He's ok with failure but doesn't stay there.

It's striving to be the best version of yourself, that God intended you to be.

WHO MADE WHO

There was a prophet named Jeremiah who found himself agonizing over insecurities when God was giving him an assignment he had never done. It's interesting because as much as he "debated" with God, God never lost his patience or became angry. He's patient with Jeremiah because, as we read, his goal was to build up Jeremiah's self-esteem.

> *The LORD gave me this message: "I knew you before I formed you in your mother's womb. Before you were born, I set you apart and appointed you as my prophet to the nations." "O Sovereign LORD," I said, "I can't speak for you! I'm too young!" The LORD replied, "Don't say, 'I'm too young,' for you must go wherever I send you and say whatever I tell you. And don't be afraid of the people, for I will be with you and will protect you. I, the LORD, have spoken!" Then the LORD reached out and touched my mouth and said, "Look, I have put my words in your mouth! Today I appoint you to stand up…" (Jeremiah 1:41-10, NLT).*

What a reassuring statement God makes to Jeremiah, which we can borrow as affirmation for ourselves. *"I knew you before I formed you in your mother's womb. Before you were born, I set you apart and appointed you".*

STAND UP

Our security and self-esteem come from the Lord in three ways as we discover in this conversation between Jeremiah and God. These will pull you out of living in insecurities and you will *"stand up"* in your self-assurance from the Lord.

Contrast

Right away Jeremiah jumps to his age comparing to the other prior prophets to disqualify himself saying, *"I'm too young!"*

If you are supposed to be like everyone else, you'd be unnecessary. You're made different for a reason. You miss out on the different, and unique, man you were created to be when comparing yourself to others. This scripture strongly encourages to do the opposite – contrast. *"We do not dare to compare ourselves with those who…measure themselves, and they judge themselves by what they themselves are. This shows that they know nothing." (2 Corinthians 10:12, NCV).*

Get to "know" the uniqueness, and greatness, God formed in you.

Confidence

Jeremiah cannot see what God sees. He is so struck with insecurity and fear he informs God what he's up against just in case He didn't know the contentious spiritual condition people were in; he might offend some. The Lord affirms his esteem by telling him, *"Don't be afraid of the people, for I will be with you and will protect you"*. Basically, He's telling Jeremiah, you're right. Your confidence is riding on me. Who argues against that?

This is where our faith grows in life, *"Confidence that we have is through Christ." (2 Corinthians 3:4, ESV).*

We look for God to work and our peace is in his ability. By the way, Christ's ability is far greater than you'll ever experience.

Competence

Jeremiah has horrible self-talk. When he considers this opportunity, he reminds God he is unqualified for the task. But God doesn't call the qualified, he qualifies the called. The Lord has a little "come to Jesus" moment and says, *"Look, I have put my words in your mouth!"*

The greatest source you will ever have for your self-assurance will be knowing, *"Our competence comes from God." (2 Corinthians 3:5)*

If he's giving you opportunities, he has equipped you to do it. It doesn't matter where you're at in your life with Christ.

HIDDEN INADEQUACIES

When I express my wrestling with inadequacy before I speak, most are surprised. Though I seem confident and clear when I'm on stage speaking, the truth is that I get very nervous before each time I speak or preach. It could be a very large crowd, a very small crowd, it doesn't matter.

Every time before I speak a couple of things take place. I have an increase of anxiety and I have a slight queasiness in my stomach. I need to use the restroom minutes before the service or event begins. And I also worry that my media presentation will fail or will not be presented correctly by the controller. I've never described all these issues before and, as I write this, I can't believe how difficult this is for me. Yeah, it gets rough, and I've been speaking on a weekly basis for more than two decades.

Where does all my tension and anxiety come from? I think about how I'm inadequate, not good enough, how I might fail, and I'm worried what others think about how I perform. What's crazy is that I love what I do. It's one of my gifts and I'll never stop doing it, as long as God allows me. Did you notice how I question my competency, my confidence dips, and begin comparing myself with what others think or consider how much better others are. So how do I push through the torment and complete my task? I remind myself it's not about me or for me. I recognize my enemy, Satan, wants to ruin God's work in my life and in the lives of others. When I take my eyes off myself and remember that I'm just a beggar telling other beggars where the food is, I begin feeling bolder and more passionate. It's about the message, not the messenger. If I needed to be like someone else, I'd be unnecessary.

When it's by God, for God, and with God, lives will be changed.

To God be the glory, great things HE has done!

ASK THE LORD

When you pray to be ok with the man you are, *Contrast, Confidence,* and *Competence* need to guide your prayer life. Your faith and boldness begin to increase because you discover God is for you, God is with you, and God is out in front of you in your uncertain moments.

An older pastor once made a simple statement about prayer I'll never forget. Take this into your conversations with the Lord. He said, "Ask the Lord for help…and he will". So simple, yet hugely hope-filled at the same time. That's a good place to start talking with the Lord.

Be fearless and secure before God and man.

COURAGE QUESTIONS

1. What is an insecurity that has caused you to doubt yourself, question your ability, or backed away from opportunities?

2. Are you overly concerned with what people think about you? Where does that come from?

3. How do you talk to, and about, yourself? Does it lean towards uplifting or downgrading?

4. How do you usually compensate for the insecurity? What is a good action step to move beyond it?

BROKEN PAST
RESILIENCE

- The Paul Struggle –

O ne of the dumbest things I've done – and will never, ever do again – happened when I was about 18 years old. I was so embarrassed and speechless, but I made the other person feel much worse. I hadn't seen my friend, who recently had a baby with her husband, in a long time. Shortly after I ran into her, I asked, "Are you pregnant again?" Yeah, you know what the answer was. She said no and I shrunk…it's all a blur and I literally can't remember how I responded.

The damage was done and there was no taking the words back, or the humiliation I caused my friend. How could I face her next time without feeling like an idiot? Act like nothing happened?

NO UNDOING

Nate's life was a success in so many ways, until it came out he was committing adultery. He was a great, well-known, and respected pastor. After decades of ministry, he found himself with a heavy weight he would carry for the rest of his life. He made the choices but now he was dealing with the consequences he didn't get to choose.

Nate committed adultery and began an affair with another lady who worked in a different department of the church. Church leaders aren't exempt from temptation, giving way to temptation, and committing moral failures…nor the disaster that follows.

The affair started with flirting, then steamrolled to a sexual relationship lasting for months. As they continued the relationship, which proved to be fueled by passion alone, they made plans of one day building a future together: leaving their spouses and families permanently. The day came when Nate's affair would be discovered and his world – along with his family's world – would come crashing down.

Though he would lose everything dear to him, Nate was in such euphoria that he was refusing to see any wrong. You see, when a minister commits a moral failure, it destroys every area and masses of people in their life. He deeply hurt his wife and children, his extended family, the people in the congregation he pastored, and his occupation as well. Nate was making the decision to move on in a new life with someone else's wife. His wife ended up divorcing him, the kids left with her. All he had, after the woman he had an affair with decided to stay with her husband, was extremely painful regrets and guilt while trying to somehow move on with his life.

How do you ever recover from something so devastating? When it's your fault, you are to blame, and no one else is responsible? When you have to carry the burden of causing so much pain, sometimes lifelong, to those you love most?

Could Nate ever be able to recover from the deep regret and guilt?

BOUNCING BACK

Regret often stems from the inability to cope with something you did or didn't do. It's a guilt we feel impossible to move past or bounce back.

You make your decisions, and your decisions make you. Your story doesn't have to be over in the wounds, guilt, or shameful things you have done. Re-read that, it *doesn't have to*. Only a resilient man takes on a massive struggle like this.

How you handle your history forms your future. How will you handle the struggle of past failures, no matter how big or small?

One thing I'm sure of is, you don't want to end up where this next guy found himself when it was too late.

HALL OF FAME PAIN

Jimmy Johnson began his football coaching career in 1965. Jimmy was a coaching icon in the sport. He coached at several universities, most notably at University of Miami from 1984-1988. In 1987 he led the Hurricanes to win the National Championship as the head coach. In 1989-1993 he was the head coach of the Dallas Cowboys where they were NFL Super Bowl Champions.

In 2021, Jimmy was elected and inducted to the National Football League Hall of Fame. On that warm August night, he was to give his induction speech. Throughout that speech he recalled all the coaches, players, wins and losses, his mottos, and speeches throughout his long career. At one point he expressed his gratitude towards his family. Mainly towards his two middle-aged adult sons in the crowd. Football coaching is taxing on the men and their families. Training and strategizing for young men and older men to beat opponents. Often spending most 24 hours working and many times sleeping on a couch in the office. As a coach in college you're constantly and intensely recruiting high school students throughout the year. You're going to their games, meeting with their parents, sending them letters, and hosting them on campus visits in order to have them attend your university and bolster your program. After doing all of this for hundreds of athletes, some he does remember and many he doesn't, he shared what he did for his sons. In his speech he disappointingly stated, "My two sons played football and I never seen them play a down". Imagine that! Your dad is the amazing Jimmy Johnson, national college champion and the NFL world champion – yet he never attends one of your games. He later stated in the speech he loved them so much and their relationship is much better now. But what a difficult memory for him, and more importantly his sons to know your dad traveled the nation to watch so many high school football players in games but he never came to yours.

My heart broke for those men when I heard Jimmy shamefully admitting his fault. A past full of regret. A past you would love to do over.

WE KNOW GOD CAN FORGIVE

In 1 John 1:9 it says, *"God is faithful and just and will forgive us"* and Jeremiah 34:31 states, *"I will forgive…and remember their sins no more"*. Many of us have heard or maybe even memorized these scriptures. This is a picture of a God who wants to love you and way more than discipline us. Immediately we can turn to him, with confession, and boom – we're all good with him. We're grateful for the forgiveness of God, but how do you and I move forward without being haunted by our guilt? God has the supernatural ability to forget about our sin, but for us the regretful things we've done are almost impossible to let go of.

Why can't we forget?

The reason we can't is because we have an evil adversary who not only keeps bringing the regrets to mind, but also continually heaps condemnation for what we've done and lies to us by making us believe God is going to pay us back eventually. It keeps this deep sting of guilt alive and kills our spirit.

Revelation 12:10 labels Satan as the *"Accuser of the brethren",* condemning us before the Lord. He's trying to ruin us by using our sin and guilt to destroy us. You know why I feel this is really hard to abandon? So many times I agree with Satan on some of the things he's saying. Accusations like "That was the last straw", "you're not forgivable", "you owe God", "you're pathetic", or "you don't deserve it". I could go on and on, and you probably can too.

Belief in these things causes us to not forgive ourselves. Sometimes *we* are personally the hardest person in the world to forgive.

How do we defeat Satan's accusations? How do we begin to self-forgive? Romans 8:1 says, *"There is therefore now no condemnation for those who are in Christ Jesus"*. This is the truth we destroy the devil's lies with. Since we chose to invite Christ as our Lord and Savior, and receive his work on the cross for us, he put an end to the condemnation of our sins forever, from the greatest to the least. Whenever you hear accusations from Satan, eliminate them with the truth of God's Word. The truth of God is what we stand on. That's where we start over.

I've done things in my life I regret, and there have been things I haven't done in my life I regret. I've embarrassed myself, inflicted pain on myself, and even made things hard for others. I recall what I may have said to someone, or the way I said it, that I'd like to have back. There have been plenty of times I've hurt people by what I didn't say when I had the chance. When I think about the way I've fathered my kids at moments, I wish I never spoke or acted in the way I did. From major life decisions and behaviors to even subtle remarks, regrets from the past can be defeating. Many times it results in us folding like lawn chairs and giving up. We don't know how to move forward in victory.

YOUR LATTER CAN BE GREATER

One of my favorite Bible characters I enjoy most is Saul, who became known as the Apostle Paul. The two names are used interchangeably as Saul was his Jewish name, and Paul was the Greek translation. He is the catalyst for the early church. He went on mission trips to start churches all around the Mediterranean Sea. He wrote 14 of the 27 books in the New Testament. It's his writings in which we continually build our faith on Christ. Eventually he was martyred for his faith.

Before doing any of these amazing things, he had a very different, violent, and ugly past. A past which we would agree there were all the reasons for him never being involved in the gospel advancing.

The book of Acts records a testimony Paul gives to Herod Agrippa, the last Jewish King in Judea, before finding his faith in Jesus Christ the Messiah.

> *"I was given a thorough Jewish training from my earliest childhood among my own people and in Jerusalem. If they would admit it, they know that I have been a member of the Pharisees, the strictest sect of our religion…I used to believe that I ought*

to do everything I could to oppose the very name of Jesus the Nazarene. Indeed, I did just that in Jerusalem. Authorized by the leading priests, I caused many believers there to be sent to prison. And I cast my vote against them when they were condemned to death. Many times I had them punished in the synagogues to get them to curse Jesus. I was so violently opposed to them that I even chased them down in foreign cities. (26:4-5, 9-11, NLT).

Perhaps the murder, by stoning, of a loyal follower and disciple of Stephen paints the picture. Acts 8:1 states, *"And Saul was there giving approval of his death".* He was part of the jeering, and shouting, anger, and indignation, justifying murder. This is who Saul was at the core.

He then has an encounter with Jesus that altered his life forever. God would give him a calling to spread the gospel to those far from God, into a saving and loving relationship with Christ.

Paul who wanted to murder Christians, or at least lock them in prison, would have a fresh start. How do you overcome the guilt and regretful thoughts of the past? Not only did Paul find the way to overcome, he shares his perspective of faith he had and we should all apply when we're in this frame of mind.

Regarding knowing Christ more, he was emphatic when he taught in Philippians 3:12-14, *"Not that I have already obtained all this, or have already been made perfect, but I press on to take hold of that for which Christ Jesus took hold of me. Brothers, I do not consider myself yet to have taken hold of it. But one thing I do: forgetting what is behind and straining toward what is ahead, I press on toward the goal to win the prize for which God has called me heavenward in Christ Jesus."*

Paul made it clear he wasn't there yet, and he wouldn't pretend to be. But he pressed on, continually without giving up, to be his best in Christ for the rest of his life until he sees Jesus face to face when he accepts his prize which is Heaven.

What was his secret to making his latter life greater than his former way of life? How did he overcome the horrific thoughts and shameful behavior we can remember from the past? He is practical and straightforward about how he is doing it and will for the rest of his life when saying, *"But one thing I do: forgetting what is behind and straining toward what is ahead"*. That's it. The only focus we need to be resilient and bounce back which is never easy work. Only fearless men can, and are willing to, have some grit. When you got fired, cheated, said something, sent the text, lied, stole, got drunk, had a one-nighter, the response must always be the same following confession, submitting to the Lord.

Your focus: *forget and strain.*

Over, and over, and over, for the rest of your life like Paul.

BROKEN DRUNKARD

I got to know Lewis, who had a heart of gold. You could always tell he was genuine when he spoke, and tender when emotional.

Lewis was a rock music artist and a believer. When his band had major hits hitting the airwaves throughout the nation and world, and concerts with world-renowned bands things got toxic. It was the riches, the drugs, women, fame, and so on. One popular band, even more well-known, would vow to Lewis's band, "We're going to show you how to party".

His band went for it, and hard. Lewis found himself always drinking. Being a rockstar affords you permission to live a life of partying and "good times". Lewis became an alcoholic over time and, due to his alcoholism while on the road, with a wife at home, started making decisions that were wrecking his life.

He openly states he was a broken man, an alcoholic who was ruining his life. He needed a savior, and he needed deliverance from his addiction. Finally, Lewis applied for, and attended a recovery group and started down the road to sobriety. He grew in his relationship with Jesus, and his family followed by placing their faith in Christ as well. He is no longer a broken man, but a man filled with hope. He could dwell on the toxic memories of the past, but he's decided to look forward and not backwards.

But it doesn't and can't end there. Lewis is intentional and determined to never return to alcoholism. He told me at any time he could go right back to it. So, you know what he does? In every city they tour, he finds the local group he belongs in and goes to the meetings.

Lewis is focused on one thing – forgetting and straining. He is committed to every straining step. He is a testimony of resilience.

OVER AND OVER AGAIN

"Formula 409" is a cleaning solution that has probably been in one of your cabinets over the years. It was invented in 1957 by Morris D. Rouff. It was finally created after many trials and effort. He, along with others, labored continuous hours trying to find the right mix of chemicals to arrive at a quality solvent. Over, and over again, they'd make a mixture, only to find out what didn't work. They tried hundreds of times to no avail. You would think at some point he would quit and settle with what he found or ditch his effort altogether. But Morris was determined to create the quality chemical he envisioned.

Finally, one day he found the right measurements of combined chemicals. He and his team recorded how many experiments to achieve the desired solvent. The final mixture was the 409th trial, thus the name "Formula 409". It took one after another after another of resilient effort to achieve what they wanted.

The same applies to us in our unfortunate history of mistakes, and failures we've endured. Each day is another experiment to "forget and strain" to have victory over the past life and rewards in the future.

UNFORESEEN CHANCE

Nate, the pastor I mentioned in the beginning of this chapter, was valiant in his effort to bounce back from his terrible behavior and damage he had caused. After moving to another city, he chose to restart his life. He grew close to the Lord and turned to him for help as he began rebuilding his life and beginning a new career. He had grit and honorable tenacity to make the best of the rest of his life. He pursued restoration of his relationship with his kids and carefully making a new connection with his then ex-wife. Because of his resilience, willing to do the small and hard things consistently, he witnessed God's hand working in the relationship with his wife. After a couple of years of reestablishing his integrity and reconstructing trust in their relationship, Nate and his wife remarried.

Stories like this don't always happen. But you never know if the next story of resilience is yours.

Fearless men are resilient.

COURAGE QUESTIONS

1. In the past, when you have failed or wrongly behaved, in some way, have you been hard on yourself? In what way?

2. What is something(s) specific you currently need to recover and develop resiliency?

3. As a resilient man, what do you believe you need to do so you move forward?

4

FATAL LABELS
IDENTITY

- The Gideon Struggle –

When I was a youth pastor, Jonathan was a student in our ministry. He was faithful and regularly attended. All the kids enjoyed being around him and he was well liked. He really enjoyed cooking and spent a lot of time in the kitchen. Jonathan would bake desserts and cook different dishes. He wasn't a strong, aggressive type of teenage boy, didn't play any sports, go hunting with his dad, or chase girls. He spent quite a bit of time hanging out with young ladies, and they shared the common interest of cooking. Another characteristic he had that made him "different" was he was somewhat softer with his gestures and didn't have a very masculine tone when he spoke. More and more I noticed Jonathan wasn't included or invited to spend time with any guys.

I discovered Jonathan was now getting the label that he was gay. He didn't ask to be categorized that way. He was just an adolescent being himself and enjoying life. He received this treatment from kids and was even perceived by teachers at school as being gay, or at least bi-sexual. This began to impact Jonathan as he grew insecure and unsure of who he was. Up to this point of adolescence, his sexuality wasn't in question, nor did he ever consider what his sexual identity would be.

THE CATEGORIES ARE

The world would tell Jonathan you're a woman in a man's body, or you must like men. Because he didn't seem to fit in with the average guy, and wasn't biologically female with shared interests, it "made sense" to others he belonged in the gay category. So, he now began to find acceptance from everyone as he embraced himself as a homosexual. This poor guy had to struggle with identity at an early age because our culture demanded so. This is all too common in our sexual world today. Because you're different, innocent, or not, you must fit into a category that culture creates and makes for you. You cannot have interests that females enjoy and be allowed to go through puberty where you grow into the identity of a young man. Our dysfunctional, secular society has dismissed room for unique individuals to be the way God made them. I think it's interesting in Jonathan's case that, as far as being a cook, most of the greatest chefs in the world are men (i.e., Gordon Ramsey, Wolfgang Puck).

The world creates havens of lies for those unsure of themselves. If you are reading this and carry this same burden as Jonathan, I want you to know, you're not alone. You don't have to hide; your freedom will come by learning who and what God designed you to be. As men our focus is to look through the eyes of God, the Bible, to determine who we are, where we belong, and how we should live.

Labels we buy into, if not God-given, can be fatal to the direction of our lives and who we believe we are.

I once heard, *"The world will ask you who you are, and if you do not know, it will tell you."* This is so true in our age today. It is crucial all men discover their divine identity to live a fulfilling and rewarding life. If we don't, we'll listen to the voices of our world as they tell us how we should be. Most men are just existing without purpose. They're wanting to know the answers to big questions such as "What's my purpose?", "What am I here for?", and "What's God's will for my life?" Since we haven't found these true answers, we live reflecting the world's lifestyle, pursuits, aimless goals, casual religion, and so on. It only makes sense we try to be a man, tough and strong, while wandering through life. Even for Christian men it is an endless search.

DEFAULT IDENTITY

There I was sitting around a table with men who were convicted of murder, or multiple murders. We were sitting in a large, cold, concrete room. My ministry had opened doors for me to disciple men in prisons, which began in Folsom State Prison in California. Most of the men I was sitting with on that particular day were incarcerated for life.

Each man took turns discussing how they ended up where they were and the decisions they made to arrive there. To my delight none of them tried to deny their guilt but owned their crime. One man opened up courageously in front of the others as I asked him to tell us about his history. He shared how his relationship with his dad made an impact on him. His dad was a tough Latino involved in gangs, a drug dealer and user, an alcoholic, and criminal. His dad would be gone for periods of times in his life, but when he was present, he enjoyed tagging along with him. At age 11, this inmate transparently shared that he used cocaine for the first time with his dad. He would be at gang parties and participate in any activities happening there. During the times his dad would disappear for a series of months, he would stay involved in this destructive life of crime, trying his best to be like his feared dad the others knew. He dropped out of school and the life of crime and drugs accelerated as he lived out his days becoming just like his father. When his dad would come back around, others would brag to the man about how his son was just like him. This is the only life of success this inmate knew. It all ended the day he found himself arrested and eventually convicted of a double homicide. He found himself enduring a life sentence, striving to know his identity and discover who he was in Christ.

We are beings designed and defined by God alone. You were created with a label that will never fade or grow old. Once you discover it, you'll never want to abandon it. My friend you are the *Imago Dei* (Latin meaning Image of God). In the world you'll learn many opinions about you but in God's word you will learn the facts about you.

How do we find our true identity? Who we are and what are we living for.

MIGHTIER THAN YOU KNOW

Gideon was a man in the Old Testament who not only lacked identity, but he also didn't know he lacked it. Therefore, he knew nothing about having personal purpose or meaning. But he would find himself learning exactly who he was and what he'd be known for. The story begins initially as a conversation with an angel, then shifts to what is called a *theophany* in Greek. (*theo*: God and *phany*: vision). These encounters occurred a handful of times in the Bible when the Christ would appear in bodily form to people. Though we may never have this type of experience, we can easily learn how God gives his image of ourselves through identity, purpose, and a mission.

> *"The angel of the LORD came and sat down under the oak in Ophrah that belonged to Joash the Abiezrite, where his son Gideon was threshing wheat in a winepress to keep it from the Midianites. When the angel of the LORD appeared to Gideon, he said, "The LORD is with you, mighty warrior." "But sir," Gideon replied, "If the LORD is with us, why has all this happened to us? Where are all his wonders that our fathers told us about when they said, 'Did not the LORD bring us up out of Egypt?' But now the LORD has abandoned us and put us into the hand of Midian." The LORD turned to him and said, "Go in the strength you have and save Israel out of Midian's hand. Am I not sending you?" "But Lord," Gideon asked, "how can I save Israel? My clan is the weakest in Manasseh, and I am the least in my family." The LORD answered, "I will be with you, and you will strike down all the Midianites together." (Judges 6:11-16)*

Later in this real-life encounter Gideon becomes the nation's leader in battle. The Spirit of the Lord comes upon him, and he defeats an army of 120,000 soldiers with 300 soldiers. Yeah, you gotta read the entire story.

What is most valuable for us as men to zero in on is the identity crisis Gideon finds himself in as he engages in this conversation with the

Lord. He's looking at his current occupation as a grain-grinder (threshing wheat), his family reputation, and his personal abilities while the Lord is calling him "Mighty Warrior". He's just minding his own business like most men; working nine to five, living for the weekend, putting food on the table, maybe attend church on a Sunday, and play on a softball team with the fellas. His main concern is correctly grinding the grain. But God knew greater and created greater inside of Gideon.

He created Gideon to live with a "fight" not a grind; like most of us default to. Every warrior has a battle to fight. Gideon's charge from God was to save Israel from the nation which had bullied them. He was fighting for the lives of people. His "fight" was his life's purpose.

What's your "fight"? What's your purpose? What is God's purpose for your life? Are you living it?

PISSED OFF

"Pissed off" is a little strong for some but let me explain.

I have a good ol' friend I'll call Frank. He was involved in church leadership for years and enjoyed ministering, teaching, and caring for people...he was called to it. He loves the Lord, and he loves people. When you get around him you just feel relaxed and at peace.

After years of church ministry something got ahold of Frank's heart like never before. He began to learn what the painful numbers and statistics were for lead pastors quitting ministry positions, failing in ministry, or leaving their calling altogether. These men and women were so exhausted giving to others, their souls had become a desolate wasteland. Finally, Frank had enough of what he was discovering, and later told a group of us as he ended sharing his findings, "It pissed me off!" He was upset this was happening and knew something must change and someone must do something. That was the season he found his lifelong "fight"; his purpose was clear.

Frank founded and launched an organization focused on replenishing lead pastors, keeping them healthy and recovering the broken. He invites pastors to all-inclusive getaways for days at a time in classy locations to relax and find encouragement. He works countless hours and travels the nation to network, find investors to pay for trips, expand the organization's team, meet more pastors, all with passion-filled purpose. He refuses to stand by and watch people hurting while pastors leave their churches in exhaustion and pain.

Frank is a mighty warrior. He's "pissed off"…for a good reason. He's got a fight.

A NATURAL BORN FIGHTER

Hear me friend, YOU are a mighty warrior. You may not see it or know it yet like Gideon, but God has put a fight in you. He's given you a purpose. I believe we ask the wrong question with, "What's my purpose?" when we should really be asking, "What needs to change?" One change is about you and the other is way bigger than you. People confuse purpose with personal success and fulfillment in their own lives. Purpose without helping people is only ambition for self. But your purpose exists for the benefit of others. We fight to make the world a better place for somebody else. We have a growing passion inspiring us to find the solution for the cure and continue to cure more. Your purpose is for understanding what could be and should be, then give your life to it. I'm telling you, no matter what your life status, past, or present has been, God has given you your own fight. It's a life-long fight God has given you and you'll never be as fulfilled doing anything else.

When you and I know our God-given purpose and live a life pursuing it, that's where we find our true-life label.

As Gideon realized his new label, he had a few things to fight through on his way to saving the nation of Israel. Each of the areas to fight give us different lenses to see how we might be able to see our own purpose revealed to us as well.

Gideon had to fight from his passion

God told him he was sending Gideon to fight with his "strength". The "strength" in this scripture comes from the Hebrew term, *Chayil*, meaning force, valor, or power. God saw the strength he created in Gideon when significance was invisible to himself.

A man named David discovered a fight within himself which began to stir a passion in him. As he grew in his relationship with the Lord, he was developing more compassion for people. He had a greater concern for those in pain. David was a small business owner but now God was calling him to get into the ring for his fight. In his mid-40s God was telling him to become a doctor! What made this so crazy is he only had an associate degree from the local community college and, if he wanted to become a doctor, he would have to become a full-time student to finish at the local university, then attend medical school. This would require years of tireless work and sleepless nights while trying to manage a small business. But why did my friend choose to spend hundreds of thousands of dollars, study hundreds of hours in books, move to another city for residency, years denying other opportunities, push through times of exhaustion and tempted to quit, and be limited to a sliver of a social life? David's fight was to help hurting and injured people which God would show him this is the route He wanted David to take. David knows this and caring for people is his passion and he is fighting for the health of people.

Jeremy is a barber. He's been cutting hair for several years. He owns his own shop, has several other barbers who work there, and guys from all over the city go to his shop to get their "fade", "ears raised", "line up", or whatever you call it. Jeremy has a sincere love for God and, if you talk to him very long about his savior, you'll find him getting choked up and emotional. As he has worked with men over the years, the more he's felt a burden for their lives. Jeremy believed he needed to, and could do, something to minister to the men even though he isn't a minister. On Monday nights, which is his day off, he opens the shop for a Bible study and gathering for men. Most Monday nights are packed out. Men from anywhere and everywhere, and all ages come to his barbershop to be discipled in the things of Christ. Jeremy knows his fight. He's fighting for men to grow in their faith in God.

Gideon had to fight from his experiences

God tells Gideon to go and save Israel even though his "clan" was the weakest. His lineage, upbringing and past disqualified him in his eyes due to him believing the fatal labels. For many men, looking at their past, especially with hurts and scars, removes potential for a real purpose. They minimize any type of impact they can make, not realizing purpose can be birthed out of the worst of circumstances. Your greatest significance in life can come from the deepest wounds in your past.

I've met many brave individuals who have decided to take the difficult and painful experiences life has dealt them to jump in, becoming a beacon of hope for others. Your ability to find personal healing and then give it away to others is a fight worth giving your life to.

Though my hurt in the past doesn't get near severe or extreme, it does serve as an example of what God can do through a broken and hurting man. My previous book, *"No More Dad Issues"*, is about the difficult relationship I had with my dad. It caused me to be a bitter person, live angrily, and strive endlessly to find approval. My relationship with my dad was my deepest hurt and one I couldn't seem to heal from. Eventually I did find healing and strength in my heart long before my dad's passing. It was freeing to know that, even though my relationship was dysfunctional with my dad for decades, I didn't live as a wounded man, but free. Months after he passed, I was encouraged to write a book about my story and what God had done in my life. It wasn't something I wanted to do because other people thought I should. I didn't even want to be an author, which I'm sure appears strange to read since you're reading my second book. Eventually the Lord would get ahold of my heart and give me vision for a book and ministry I never would have guessed. Not only did I write that book, I went on to start a non-profit organization to help people heal from dad issues and help dads become heroes. I'm in this fight for the long-haul. I'm fighting to see generations healed of father wounds and it's happening.

If you've endured and healed from abuse in any form, consider how God may want to use it for your greater healing and changing the lives of others. Your past misery can become your future ministry. If you have something you're hiding or struggling with, just remember you're not alone.

Gideon had to fight from his status

Gideon makes some good arguments with God. At least they were good arguments to him. He brought up several reasons, and labels, to explain why he wasn't a warrior. Making it clear he wasn't the guy for the fight. He was fixed on the label of being "the least"; not enough and good for nothing.

Joaquin had a rough teenage life. As he spent more time running the streets than he did with family, he got caught up in the drug world. He would try various forms of drugs and eventually become an addict. He then began to sell drugs and became a popular dealer in the city. He made a lot of money and used many drugs in his teens, 20s, and 30s. In his mid-30s he came to Christ, was delivered from drugs, and left his former life. Joaquin grew in the Bible, his faith, and church family. He adjusted to a life of a normal citizen, earning a paycheck instead making drug deals for money he didn't need. Over time he began to see the transformation in his life and the riddance of decades of addictions and wanted to help others. He found a fight, sharing his testimony with others in recovery and serving as a counselor. He found a way to use his past to help others and fuel a purpose God had planned for him. He's fighting for others to get set free from addiction.

Another man was his worst enemy. He had been successful over the early years of marriage. He was a multimillionaire. They enjoyed all the fancy trips, cars, and jewelry just like anyone else would. But things wouldn't last very long. Though he made a lot of money, he had created debt in the millions as well. After making horrible money decisions, to say the least, he would end up losing everything including their home and the furniture inside and eventually declared bankruptcy with nothing to his name. He made the tough commitment to the Lord that he would handle all his finances and solve his debt crisis the way God commanded. He got out of debt and has since become financial life coach to many. Dave Ramsey knows his fight. From his radio show to the Financial Peace University program and his organization, he is passionate about people finding freedom from debt and building personal wealth. He is a mighty warrior.

ONLY ONE HAS THE RIGHT

What's gonna be your fight? God sees a fight deep within you that most don't. Your God-given fight, purpose, will be who you are and what you're known for. Man cannot re-label what God has created… unless you allow it.

> *"For we are God's [own] handiwork (His workmanship), recreated in Christ Jesus, [born anew] that we may do those good works which God predestined (planned beforehand) for us [taking paths which He prepared ahead of time], that we should walk in them [living the good life which He prearranged and made ready for us to live]." (Ephesians 2:10, AMP).*

When we give our lives to Christ, we discover the plans and preparations God has made for each of us. Without Christ you never get to learn the "handiwork" of God on your life and the uniqueness he's created you with. Your sexual identity, professional identity, social identity and so on have no value outside of the divine design of God. The only way you'll ever find lasting fulfillment and satisfaction is turning to the heart of God. It's there you'll find YOUR label, YOUR fight, and YOUR victory!

Gideon's unrealized identity and purpose began with his time with God. Your "fight" is found in the Lord. Take a timeout, push pause, or blow the whistle to ask God "What's my fight?", "Who am I to fight for?" It's not about you finding personal success. Ask God to reveal the burden he's created within you that will benefit others.

Go pick your fight Mighty Warrior.

COURAGE QUESTIONS

1. Have you wrongly identified yourself outside of how God identifies you? Why?

2. What is the fight you are passionate about and willing to do something to bring change? Describe.

3. What is a practical way, like the examples given, you can develop your purpose and fight?

5

SUPERSIZE ME
CONTENTMENT

- The Judas Struggle –

Me and my wife were on a wonderful trip in Rome, Italy. We visited all the historical sites over a three-day period and enjoyed true Italian pizza each of those days. We loved going to the Vatican and walking to the top of its dome to see all of Rome. Then there was St. Peter's Basilica, the Colosseum, and so much more. What I enjoyed daily was getting espresso when visiting the corner cafes each morning and throughout the day. Usually I get an "Americano" in our country, so it was a little challenge getting my usual just right. The biggest dilemma I had was the size of the cups they use for the coffee. The little cups, which seemed just a tad larger than a Dixie cup, were just one to two gulps for me and I was used to getting a Venti at my local Starbucks. I kept trying to get them to put it in a larger cup, but they had none. Finally, I was a little annoyed and asked them to just make me two cups and I headed out double fisted. When I walked to the cashier a little old Italian lady sat there, who had overheard my interaction from a distance, began to ring me up. As I paid, she seemed to roll her eyes, and I tried to explain to her I like larger. Then she said in slightly broken English, "That's why all you Americans are fat. You want everything big." She made me feel like an American idiot. I then laughed, and it caused me to think how other countries give smaller portions of food and drinks while we have to "supersize" almost everything.

As men, when it comes to money, possessions, and material things we want to go "supersize".

Our society taps into this weakness we have. Commercials and ads run while we enjoy shows more on the masculine side. After we have engaged with a certain ad on social media, algorithms generate products related to what we've viewed and more pop up on our feeds. Prices are geared to push you to a larger quantity of whatever you want. Our culture knows this about men, that we have an appetite for, you guessed it, more.

We can easily become discontented with what we have as we compare it to something greater and find ourselves in the place of dissatisfaction. We're convinced the way we find contentment within, satisfaction with what we have, and not wanting more, is to acquire more. The problem is "more" doesn't have an end. When you get more, eventually we'll want even more…many times for no reason.

IMAGE IS EMPTY

Derek is a suburban father and husband and has a public profession for his occupation. His wife is a terrific lady, one to be admired. He's got a great spirit about him, and people love him. But Derek has a problem which is damaging his marriage and creates tension in the home financially.

Derek desires to be seen as a successful man, one that others would want to be like. He appears to be one of the most influential among the fellas. While his wife has a good running, well-kept, and modest car, he has much more. He has two cars for himself and a couple other recreational vehicles, some of which still have payments. Not only did he refuse to sell any to minimize monthly financial obligations, but he also made some of these large purchases without mentioning them to his wife.

What now compounds this lifestyle he cannot afford is he has to make more money. Now Derek finds himself working a lot of overtime hours so he can keep up the image. Derek is in search of a content life but continues to dig himself and his family deeper into a pit due to his discontentment. He doesn't know how to have contentment and a great image simultaneously. Is the pursuit of more really making life better?

While he appears to be a financial success to others with his possessions, he is failing to have a trusting relationship with his wife. When will Derek stop needing to impress others? Fearless men don't excuse this lifestyle away but will evaluate their hearts and not justify the strain, debt, collection of toys, and excessive work hours.

The fear Derek's wife has is that he will continue to buy more.

DREAM BIG

After 10 years of owning our home in California, we gained a large amount of equity. It was a time when local people were experiencing the same. Many people began selling their homes and buying newer, bigger homes, in better areas. As we witnessed the real estate action increasing and people making upgrades, that idea began to enter our thoughts and lead us to consider doing it as well. Conversations about this continued for a period. Everyone was acquiring their "dream home" while we were just staying in ours.

Finally, one day it dawned on me, and I told my wife, "We have our dream home". Leading up to buying the house we currently lived in, it had everything we desired in a home. I recalled how we made a list of things we wanted and needed in our home, and the neighborhood we really wanted to live in. We knew how many rooms were necessary, we had a special layout in mind, having a porch out front, and so on. As I continued talking with my wife, I shared that our house has everything we desired and wanted. Suddenly we were wanting to walk away to have "more"; whatever that was. It was then we pulled back and understood we were content with where we were. At the time of writing this book we have lived in this fine home close to 20 years. We've never once been unhappy with it or our neighborhood.

Most people who were buying and selling were not only moving into larger homes, but they were also building larger debt and mortgage payments. How long were they content with this standard of living?

SAY WHEN

Friend, when will enough be enough? When will you have a "good salary"? How long will you be ok with the standard of living it produces? Stop and process that for a minute and be honest with yourself.

At what point will you be ok not getting more toys, going on big vacations, and wearing fine jewelry and clothing for you to "feel" satisfied? You may be able to afford all of these fine things, but are you acquiring these things because, if you're not gaining more, you're unsettled in your spirit?

What do you buy regularly? How would you feel never buying another? When will you have a limit? When will you be content and satisfied?

A coach, four-time super bowl champion and National Football League Hall of Famer, Deion "Prime Time" Sanders openly shares, *"I tried everything. Parties, women, buying expensive jewelry and gadgets, and nothing helped. There was no peace. I had everything the world has to offer, but no peace, no joy, just emptiness inside"*. There was never enough to remove the emptiness and discontentment in his life.

Deion found himself living a life of sin trying to find contentment. Its origin was found in money as 1 Timothy 6:10 explains, *"For the love of money is a root of all kinds of evil. Some people, eager for money, have wandered from the faith and pierced themselves with many griefs."* This isn't referring to a mere piece of paper but everything that involves money; the eagerness to have and get it, the idol it becomes, the pleasures coming from what it provides, and so forth. This cycle continues, if we remain discontent, and can lead us away from our trust in the Lord and to painful results. This is what greed does.

You can be content or discontent. Which "tent" will you live in?

PAINFULLY GREEDY

Judas Iscariot didn't magically appear one day as a greedy betrayer of Jesus. It was a gradual descent of discontentment turning into greed.

Many are quick to say they're not greedy, but greed is an excessive desire for more. Psychologist Erich Fromm defines greed as, *"a bottomless pit which exhausts the person in an endless effort to satisfy the need without ever reaching satisfaction."* It comes from the heart and varies in how it reveals itself in individuals. Judas, void of wisdom and driven by his longing to have more, eventually blurred his eyes to betray Christ.

In John's gospel, he explains who Judas was during the extravagant act of worship a woman who used an expensive fragrance to wash the feet of Jesus. *"But Judas Iscariot, one of his disciples—the one who would betray him—said, 'That perfume was worth a fortune. It should have been sold and the money given to the poor.' Not that he cared for the poor, but he was in charge of the disciples' funds and often dipped into them for his own use!"* (John 12:4-6, TLB). The NIV version says Judas used to *"help himself"*. Out of greed, desire to have to increase grew little by little, taking some here and taking some there from the disciples. He even tried to disguise his greed by pointing out the woman should have given to the poor.

Ultimately after Judas did the unthinkable, betraying Jesus, to make some extra money, turned into deadly remorse.

Matthew 27:3-5 explains, *"When Judas, who had betrayed him, saw that Jesus was condemned, he was seized with remorse and returned the thirty silver coins to the chief priests and the elders. 'I have sinned,' he said, 'for I have betrayed innocent blood.' 'What is that to us?' they replied. 'That's your responsibility.' So, Judas threw the money into the temple and left. Then he went away and hanged himself"*. Judas was captured and taken hostage by a remorse he would never get free from. Though none of us will betray Jesus, greed, if left unaddressed, will bring regret and remorse in some areas of our lives eventually.

EXHAUSTING WEALTH

An empty, dissatisfying life in pursuit of more things is a laborious life. Proverbs 23:4 (NLT) states, *"Don't wear yourself out trying to get rich. Be wise enough to know when to quit."* Striving to have more possessions, paychecks, or flash will wear you out eventually. It will take its toll in a handful of ways: worry and anxiety due to payments to be made, relational strains like Derek had with his wife, spiritually as we have made an idol, and laboring more to have enough money in the bank account.

How do you arrive at a place of contentment? It requires one main ingredient. The previous scripture tells us men to *"Be wise to know when to quit"*. Know your limits, know your fleshly desires, and know your responsibilities. This path to contentment is paved with the decision to use wisdom. Your commitment to this decision will eventually override your emotions to have more things. I often say, *feelings follow behavior.*

Your decisions concerning money, possessions, and pleasures will determine your direction, discontentment, or contentment.

LOYALTY IN QUESTION

Money, and all it provides, is going to have an impact on our relationship with God, who is the only source of true contentment and satisfaction. Matthew 6:24 is a popular scripture outlining the struggle. Money is going to test our loyalty to God; if he owns our heart or if money does. *"No one can serve two masters. Either he will hate the one and love the other, or he will be devoted to the one and despise the other. You cannot serve both God and Money."* Money is the number one competitor for your heart. You will chase after one of these things, only you decide. How do we measure this?

Jeremy was a faithful follower of Christ. He attended church every Sunday and any midweek event happening. He served on a weekly basis in the church in a variety of roles. I admired his personal devotional life; he is a true disciple. One area he struggled with for years was tithing ten percent of his income to the church as Malachi 3 tells us. He would try, then he'd stop, and this was a seesaw battle for him for years. The day came when he finally paid off his car after five years. It was still in good condition and ran well. After celebrating he then told me what he was going to do next. He said he was going to start looking for a new car to buy. He was ready to set up another monthly payment, even though he had a car that was sufficient. I asked him why he wanted a new car when the current car was fine. He really didn't have an answer (knowing deep down a new car would give him new enjoyment). I proceeded to tell him this is a great opportunity to begin tithing faithfully to the Lord and be loyal to Him like he was loyal to the bank. This mentality of being content with what he had was new to him. He, not I, made the decision to forego buying a new car, to tithe every month to God and he never stopped. He doesn't have any regrets, but senses a greater trust and loyalty to God, and even suggests to others they should do it too.

TUG-O-WAR

Jeremy had this tug-o-war between God and money. He was the only one to decide who could win. Obviously just because you tithe it, doesn't mean you won't struggle with contentment. But tithing is the way we testify to God and ourselves, he has our heart and money doesn't.

A very large number of Christian men don't tithe, won't tithe, or make excuses why they can't. As a pastor I've heard them all. Men tend to think of their money as their own and see tithing as robbing them from enjoying the fruits of their labor. Now they won't say that, but these are the thrusts of what lie beneath the surface. When we commit our lives to Christ it also includes our finances. My money isn't mine, it's all God's and whatever he wants me to do with his money I will. See, he must be Lord over your money. You and I just become stewards.

There's one argument I've many men make which refers to tithing as an Old Testament practice, and we no longer live under it in the New Testament. I want to give clarity as one who does give ten percent on every penny. Jesus made it clear in Matthew 23:23 tithing was to continue to be a spiritual practice. The religious leaders were using the practice of tithing to neglect giving anything to those in need so Jesus hits it hard with them without mincing words. Jesus says to them, *"Hypocrites! For you are careful to tithe even the tiniest income from your herb gardens, but you ignore the more important aspects of the law—justice, mercy, and faith. You should tithe, yes, but do not neglect the more important things."* Do you see that? Godly men should tithe and not neglect caring for people in need too! If you were to practice the habit of tithing, you would experience a sense of contentment immediately…and it would grow.

Don't be afraid of "not having enough", or delay saying, "when I can afford it". Fearless men just take a stand on God's Word, obey it, and rid themselves of many griefs. I dare you to tithe if you don't already.

I don't want or get anything from you…you already bought my book! I want something *for* you.

You're going to blessed in your spirit and in your loyalty to God.

COURAGE QUESTIONS

1. Do you believe you have lived discontent and dissatisfied in your financial life? Explain why or why not.

2. What are the treasures and pleasures you have a weakness towards? In what ways are these weaknesses having a negative impact?

3. How did you feel about tithing and its ability to bring you into a life of contentment? Do you agree or disagree?

6

WASTED POTENTIAL
OBEDIENCE

- The King Saul Struggle –

J ulius was very talented and skilled in his profession. Others in his line of work would make sacrifices to join him in the various projects he worked on and travel to the location he would be at work. His reputation for having great ability and success in his business were well known. Those who collaborated alongside him and assisted him loved being around Julius, even in social settings. It seemed as if everybody loved him…which was true, unless you were a direct supervisor he reported to.

Julius was difficult to manage if you had authority over him and his department. Because he was successful, he was always a welcomed commodity for any organization in his profession. He was so gifted it went to his head. He didn't feel he had to answer to anybody, and his attitude became one of which he believed they should be grateful they had him as an employee. He didn't like to be checked on, receive direction for his work, or give updates on progress. Whenever he didn't want to do something, it showed. Either he would put a task off and make managers wait, or do part of it and not finish it. Finally, things came to a head at an organization he was working for.

His boss, who was growing impatient and stressed by the responses of Julius, gave him a project which was a slight challenge but was not out of the reach of Julius, given the skills he possessed. Julius was given a few months, which was more than enough time, to finish the project. As his boss asked for updates each month, Julius would give a short affirmative answer but looked annoyed at the same time. Finally, the day came when he was to make his presentation in his boss's office. The manager was surprised to see Julius in the office with nothing to present. He immediately asked where the presentation was, and why didn't he come prepared. Julius's response was simply, "You're making me do something I don't do. So, I decided I'm not going to do it."

As you might have guessed, Julius's tenure didn't last beyond that day. His role was terminated, and he went on to another organization... then another...then another. Because Julius didn't like to obey orders, he couldn't sustain a job.

His unwillingness to obey has resulted in Julius's potential not fully reached.

WASTED POTENTIAL

Ezekiel was in his sixties when I occasionally met him and his wife for coffee. We would talk church ministry and he enjoyed contributing his thoughts and ideas. He had a very good handle on the way a healthy church should conduct itself. I would share different things happening and welcomed his feedback. We had a lot of fun and I trusted Ezekiel.

One time over coffee I mentioned that he should be in ministry in some degree of leadership due to his natural discernment for caring for people. As I shared that I could tell something inside of Ezekiel was churning, and with it followed eyes welling up with tears. I just encouraged him to talk to me and tell me what was going on. As his wife observed, she knew exactly what he was wrestling with – and had wrestled for years.

Ezekiel began to share about the time when God's Spirit spoke to him as a young child, and he was called into full time ministry. He described the unique moment of God describing his calling and how he was reminded throughout childhood. This was confirmed in a variety of ways over the years throughout his teens into his twenties. Yet there he was, a senior citizen, and heartbroken that he never answered God's call on his life. His response to God's Divine Call was disobedience.

As godly men, we're supposed to obey God's call, not just pick a response. Vague responses leave us room for options, timetables, and convenience. This is not how God wants us to "respond" to the great calls on for our lives. He calls for immediate, swift, and complete obedience.

Ezekiel eventually began to serve in the church in greater ways as the opportunities arose. As we see in a man in his sixties, it's never too late to start walking in obedience.

Disobedience to the Lord is where many men fall off and get bored with faith, thus most have a religion void of power. We just don't give full obedience. When obedience – giving control of what I do and letting God decide – is completely practiced there is not a better, wide open, and exciting life to live. I guarantee you will never get bored and just go through the religious rituals.

THE DANGEROUSLY REWARDING LIFE

Shortly after writing my first book, I was out on a prayer walk and heard the Lord clearly speak to me. It wasn't one of those times when he speaks encouragement and comfort, his voice commanded me to do something dangerous and filled with risk.

I felt a change of some sort, stirring within me for a couple months, not related to my book but more about me and the church I pastored. As I asked God to tell me what he wanted I received a divine prompting in my spirit from him saying, "I want you to resign. I want you to resign with nothing." Yeah, that freaked me out and, somehow, gave me rest at the same time.

Over the next few weeks God would give me confirmation and direction to move forward and walk with our church, which we started 15 years prior, through the change as well. I have been blessed with an amazing wife who willingly follows the Lord's voice, and we have journeyed together on this dangerous venture. We put everything on the line, with no salary, no job, only to trust he would provide.

Immediately after I left my position, God began to show himself faithful to the obedience he required of me. I began to receive calls and text messages from pastors asking me to speak at their retreats, conferences, Sunday services, and more. A month after leaving the church, God birthed a vision in me to form a non-profit ministry. Now we are helping hundreds of struggling dads to improve their skills and strengthen their families. The story continues to expand as we trust God in obedience. I'm not saying it hasn't been filled with challenges, fears, and facing my insecurities.

What I've learned, and continue to learn, is that obedience is not easy. It is extremely hard, dangerous, risky, irrational, and tests my pride. I don't profess to be a great man of obedience, but all I do is try so hard to surrender my security and receive his reward. I'll never regret these audacious decisions to trust and obey God. I confidently believe that obeying God with our lives is the most extreme, adventurous, and rewarding life you could ever live. And I want to see more.

There is an amazing spiritual experience following decisions of men to obey God because we are mobilizing our faith. Our faith level is demonstrated by our obedience level. Author John Maxwell commented, *"Most Christians are educated way beyond their obedience level"*. Obedience to God is not mere agreement with God. There are many Christian men who agree with God but do little with what he says, either through the prompting of His Spirit or His Word. In James 2:17 (Weymouth NT) we're told, *"Faith, if it is unaccompanied by obedience, has no life in it."* Take this to heart, when you leave off obeying God, your faith will begin to die off, Christianity will only be a boring set of rituals, while wasting the potential God has given you.

FORFEITING POTENTIAL

Why do we struggle obeying? One word, control. We are afraid of not having control and hesitate trusting God's control. Obedience says I put my life in God's control and release my plans to him.

Disobedience is a life risk and deceives us because the cost is on the backend. The cost is the consequences for not obeying God. There are two avenues in which we become disobedient in our faith resulting in sin. We have sin of commission, doing what God tells us not to do, and the sin of omission, not doing what God tells us to do.

- The sin of omission is when we know God is telling us to share our faith, foregoing the fishing trip for mission trip, forgive, serving at church instead of showing up and counting minutes to leave, praying for others, stop listening to ungodly music, bring a friend to church, breakoff the sexual relationship, but we don't.
- The sin of commission is when God is telling us not to tell the joke, take the second look, talk about the coworker, attend the event, quit the high paying job to spend more time with your family, cut out the foul language, but we do it anyway.

This sin of disobedience will cause us to waste our life's potential God has designed for each of us. If you forego obeying God, you will forfeit your potential from God. We see this exact thing happen in the life of King Saul when he forfeited God's plan for his own.

In first Samuel we witness the culmination of King Saul's decisions not to obey God and what it would cost him. King Saul was commanded to go out and destroy the pagan Amalekites and their king. In his story we will learn how easy it is to disobey, which will also teach us how to obey and discover God's will for our lives.

> "Saul and the army spared Agag and the best of the sheep and cattle, the fat calves and lambs—everything that was good. These they were <u>unwilling</u> to destroy completely, but everything that was despised and weak they totally destroyed. Then the word of the LORD came to Samuel: "I am grieved that I have made Saul king, because he has turned away from me and <u>has not carried out my instructions.</u>" Samuel was troubled, and he cried out to the LORD all that night. Early in the morning Samuel got up and went to meet Saul, but he was told, "Saul has gone

to Carmel. There he has set up a monument in his own honor and has turned and gone on down to Gilgal." When Samuel reached him, Saul said, "The LORD bless you! I have carried out the LORD's instructions." But Samuel said, "What then is this bleating of sheep in my ears? What is this lowing of cattle that I hear?" Saul answered, "The soldiers brought them from the Amalekites; they spared the best of the sheep and cattle to sacrifice to the LORD your God, but we totally destroyed the rest." "Stop!" Samuel said to Saul. "Let me tell you what the LORD said to me last night." "Tell me," Saul replied. Samuel said, "Although you were once small in your own eyes, did you not become the head of the tribes of Israel? The LORD anointed you king over Israel. And he sent you on a mission, saying, 'Go and completely destroy those wicked people, the Amalekites; make war on them until you have wiped them out.' Why did you not obey the LORD? Why did you pounce on the plunder and do evil in the eyes of the LORD?" "But I did obey the LORD," Saul said. "I went on the mission the LORD assigned me. I completely destroyed the Amalekites and brought back Agag their king. The soldiers took sheep and cattle from the plunder, the best of what was devoted to God, in order to sacrifice them to the LORD your God at Gilgal." But Samuel replied: "Does the LORD delight in burnt offerings and sacrifices as much as in obeying the voice of the LORD? To obey is better than sacrifice, and to heed is better than the fat of rams." (15:9-22).

What God expects of us is complete obedience, which is doing what is right in His eyes and not what's good in our eyes. Samuel tells King Saul, *"To obey is better than sacrifice…"* When it comes to following God's will, Samuel is communicating, good is the enemy of right. It's like me telling my son to clean his room but he goes out and mows the lawn, then proudly declares he obeyed. No, he didn't, he did a good thing but disobeyed me.

Why is it important we obey God in every detail? Because that is precisely the degree in which God desires to give us detailed blessings and living in His will. So, the enemy will deceive us to miss obedience and miss God's blessing. Here are some ways we get led astray from obeying God completely.

False Obedience

> *"But I did obey the LORD...I completely destroyed the Amalekites and brought back Agag their king".*

Saul somehow believed, and probably convinced himself, he performed complete obedience, but it just wasn't the case. Maybe he thought he had a better idea, or could bend the rules, but he lacked true and total obedience. It's easy for us men to elevate our perspective and preference over conviction to completely obey.

Partial Obedience

> *"...they were <u>unwilling</u> to destroy completely."*

Saul and his men at some point decided they weren't going to finish the job. It wasn't an accident, nor did it slip their minds, they willfully did as much as they wanted. Sometimes we arrive in this place because we don't want anyone to think they can tell us what to do...even if it's coming from God.

Slow Obedience

> *"He...has not carried out my instructions."*

Saul and his men delayed completing the mission to the point God mentions, they're not finished. It's not on our time schedule or when we want, but when God says. Some feel the need to show passive aggressiveness, or stubbornness because they perceive they are giving up control.

Good Obedience

"Saul and the army spared Agag and…everything that was good."

Saul chose to save the good stuff to give an offering to God. That was a good idea, but it was wrong. If you choose to live a life of obedience, do exactly what and how you're told, to honor God.

False, Partial, Slow, and *Good* obedience are all disobedience. Obedience doesn't change plans, leave tasks unfinished, decide timetables, or choose a different option. Why? Because it is all disobedience. Since King Saul preferred to carry out instructions on his own terms, he lost his position, authority, and wasted his potential. God revoked what he had once given King Saul, simply due to disobedience. He forfeited the full potential God had planned.

Hear me friend, these concepts of obedience are where we water down faith. When we live a fully obedient life, we will possess confidence we're in a place for God to trust and bless us with more. You will discover more and more of God's plan for your life.

MAN'S GREATEST UNANSWERED QUESTION

It's one of the most common questions all pastors are asked. It is also everyone's deep desire to have answered. This is man's greatest question:

"What is God's will for my life?" The answer is simple, but the process is difficult.

If you want to want to know what God's ultimate, lifelong will is for your life you can have it. It all hinges on your obedience. The starting point and practice is to obey God in everything His Spirit tells you, the Bible tells you, and any instructions you receive from leaders. This is my answer to every person: "God's will is for you to obey him completely today then tomorrow and so on." As days turn into months then years, you are keen to obey and will hear God's voice clearer to learn His ways and His will is more evident. When you take these strides, you will progressively see God's purpose and your potential coming together reinforcing your confidence you are living in His will for your life. As you're faithful to his plan, while abandoning yours, you'll find yourself living the abundant life he promised you. Which means, God's will and your potential are both in your hands; will they be fulfilled or wasted? Some want God to reveal plans then they'll start moving, at least they think that will be the case, but they have wasted their potential in the end.

The life of obedience will be the most dangerous, risky, on the edge of your seat life if you're willing to fearlessly live it out. If God is telling you to serve, then serve. If he's telling you to speak up about your faith, speak up. If he's saying to pray for someone, then pray for them. If he's directing you to start a new business that benefits the kingdom, well, get to work.

THE DAILY TASK

The first miracle of Jesus happened at a wedding in a town called Cana. They ran out of wine and Mary, the mother of Jesus, knew he was able to perform a miracle. Most know Jesus turned the water into wine, but before that occurred something practical happened.

Following a brief interaction she has with Jesus, Mary turns to a handful of men and says, "Do whatever he tells you." When they did so, a miracle they participated in happened before their eyes.

Friend, if you want to see God working in your life and know His will for you, don't waste your potential obeying your own desires and options. Just take the advice from Mary.

"Do whatever he tells you."

?

COURAGE QUESTIONS

1. Have you been intentional about obeying God daily, according to His Word? Would others close to you agree or disagree with you and why?

2. How do you feel about obeying God to every minute detail? Do you think it's too extreme?

3. Are you currently living up to your full potential? What needs to happen for you maintain it?

7

CHASING WIND
FULFILLMENT

- The Solomon Struggle –

There I was, sitting in my counselor's office, trying to figure out an answer to a question she posed. I was puzzled, perplexed, and uncertain of what to say. I had never been asked this basic question in all my life.

"Do you think you're successful?"

Those five words caused me to sit in silence. They triggered questions to run through my mind such as: What is success? How do you know if you are successful? What would people think if they heard me answer yes? Do people view me as successful?

My answer was that I don't know, which she followed up with "why?" I began jogging through my mind past achievements, accolades, and recognition I'd received. There seemed to be few. I thought about what I was currently doing, and if I reached any level of success (I was a lead pastor for over 15 years). I didn't feel successful. I didn't feel accomplished. I had so much more to do, didn't think I wasn't doing enough, and if I looked at how others were doing, I wasn't a success. So, I told her "I don't think I am, and I don't know why".

I believe we as men want to be known as successful; first in our own eyes, then our family's, and sadly, mostly people on the outside of our home. We work hard to arrive at that status, then the goal posts move and we're back at square one trying to "be somebody". All the while, as we are striving to be successful, we are leaving a trail of dysfunction. It could be our wives and kids who are neglected by us. We find ourselves accumulating debt. We want the approval from people who, five years later, won't be in our lives. We're consumed believing the myth, "Someday when I'm successful, I'll be important".

We have bought into the lie our self-worth and value are defined by how we perform and what we achieve. And we will give almost anything to have it.

A FAILING SUCCESS

Henry was distraught and didn't know what to do about his failing marriage and the emotional state his children were naturally feeling because of it. He wanted things to improve but didn't know what was causing the trouble and certainly didn't know how to fix it.

He shared with me the stressors in their relationship. He was spending money carelessly and she was keeping a separate account because she didn't trust him. He believed she was hiding money because she might have a relationship with another man. She was upset as she was convinced all the responsibilities for the kids were hers to bear alone, while working a full-time job herself. He believed working extra hours at work was noble and it was up to the man to provide a "good life" for his family. Henry's kids used to run to the door to see their dad but then they went into hiding when they heard the key unlock the front door. After a long 12-hour shift, he would come home exhausted only to be met with, in his mind, whiny kids and an ungrateful wife. He was frustrated and would rather be at work. She loathed when he would walk in the door because he had a short fuse, would go into a rage and yell at anyone, sometimes with foul language, then isolate himself from them in another room. They stopped going to church and keeping Christ the center of their lives – and their family was suffering because of it. She was ready to take the kids and leave him. It was a mess and going downhill fast.

Henry went on to tell me how things at work were going great. He was one of the lead men in the local branch and had been well respected for over two decades. His pay was well over six figures, and he was trusted to adjust his own hours in the 24-hour branch where he supervised hundreds of employees. Things couldn't have been better, coworkers liked working with him, and his bosses wished they had more employees like him. He put in extra hours at his job even though he wasn't required to, but it made others admire his loyalty to the company. He was an all-star at work, but when he went home, he felt like a loser and a failure.

Does this sound familiar to you? Everything outside of your home is clicking and you are really accomplishing great things, but your home is dysfunctional. Maybe you feel your career is really coming together but you somehow can't rid yourself of the emptiness stuck in your gut. You watch yourself needy for attention and approval so you're striving endlessly to have more. You're away from home constantly, playing in softball and bowling leagues, or always out with the fellas because you dread going home to tension.

I helped Henry understand something he hadn't considered before. While he was the "success guy" at work, he couldn't figure out why he wasn't a successful husband and father. He had to decide, what's more important? What's causing the most pain? What needs the most attention? Who were most valuable in his life? I told him, "while you're climbing the ladder of success it's leaning against the wrong wall." He was trying to have a sense of success, but he was unsuccessful at home. If he chose to be a success at home by investing time and energy into those relationships, cutting back on work, and stopping pursuing status, his marriage and family would be incredibly successful.

I was proud to see Henry's sincere response to make changes, put his family first, cut back at work, and ignored the chatter from others about him not being who he used to be. Henry worked hard to make adjustments for those closest to be happy, thus he would eventually see his marriage strengthen.

Henry fought the strong temptation to search for his worth in recognition, achievements, and promotions.

DRIVEN BY AFFLICTION

I walked into a college football team meeting the night before one of the biggest games in the university's history. All the players, coaches, and staff found their seats to hear a motivational speech in the gathering. The head coach invited a wealthy business alumnus to share about his life, and who he had become, to inspire these young men. He began by detailing the education and degrees he had received while attending the university. Then he transitioned to describe the long journey he took over the decades as he chased success. There he was a millionaire and a powerful man in his profession. He had made it and he assured them they could too. But something he stated, several times, caught my attention.

Over the course of the speech this boisterous and confident man referred to the source of his motivation to be successful. The thrust for his drive to perform and pursue success was found in the desertion he and his mom encountered when his father walked out and left them for good. His goal was to show his dad he could make a better life for himself than his father could ever provide. He'd declare accomplishments while each time referring to his father in a derogatory way. There was a clear bitterness and disdain towards his father which even showed itself in the expletives he used regarding his dad. This man, who appeared to be so bold and powerful, was actually wounded and hurt trying to live a life that would hopefully heal his heart.

He was tormented by an unhealthy perspective; if he performed well, he was a success and if he underperformed or underachieved, he was a failure. What a difficult way to live. Living with tension and pressure to be successful and anything else is a loss. I must admit I have found myself do the very same thing.

For those of us who have voluntarily applied this pressure on ourselves there's a common thread we share – anxiety. I was initially defensive and offended by this concept.

Through numerous surveys taken, anxiety has been a common trait of high performers and successful people suffering from it, as a driving force. I know, I know, for those of us who are make it happen, business builders, and find themselves dismissing this idea, this article provides the truth. Harvard Business Review writes, *"A surprising number of extremely successful people are wracked with anxiety. They suffer from feelings of instant negativity, worry, and doubt—what psychologists call thought traps….in workplaces, anxiety has been a hidden problem—there in plain sight, but often ignored. To combat thought traps, many anxious achievers turn to overwork."*

Success and performance are fueled by an internal fuel of fearing failure, falling short, perfectionism, and more. Why? Due to negative experiences. In elementary school, maybe you were the last player picked on the playground and nobody cared if you were on their team. Or you were made fun of, or parents called you names like "stupid" or "good for nothing". Sometimes people grow up with nothing, below the poverty level, and they fear living in that way as an adult. Our parents can be a source of anxiety, pressuring us to be perfect and were only pleased with you if you did well. Many people are afraid of letting others down or need the approval from others. What a stressful way to live just so we can feel a sense of worth and value.

WORTH THE WORK

King Solomon, who is noted to be the wisest king ever, explored the idea of success, performance, and hard work being the ultimate life worth living. Would achievements and accomplishments add the most value to life causing one to feel complete?

In Ecclesiastes 2:4-11 (NLT) Solomon describes his efforts to be a successful man, identify the definition of success, and find a strong sense of self-worth from his hard work and what it provides.

> *"I also tried to find meaning by building huge homes for myself and by planting beautiful vineyards. I made gardens and parks, filling them with all kinds of fruit trees. I built reservoirs to collect the water to irrigate my many flourishing groves. I bought slaves, both men and women, and others were born into my household.*

85

I also owned large herds and flocks, more than any of the kings who had lived in Jerusalem before me. I collected great sums of silver and gold, the treasure of many kings and provinces. I hired wonderful singers, both men and women, and had many beautiful concubines. I had everything a man could desire! So, I became greater than all who had lived in Jerusalem before me, and my wisdom never failed me…I even found great pleasure in hard work, a reward for all my labors. But as I looked at everything I had worked so hard to accomplish, it was all so meaningless—like chasing the wind. There was nothing really worthwhile anywhere."

Solomon became greater than everyone, profited much from his labor, and reached the pinnacle of success only to learn, it's not worth it. Twelve times the letter "I" is mentioned as he details all he worked for and searched for. There's no mention of family or finding wholeness. It was a saddening, empty pursuit. Like trying to catch wind, meaningless and nothing worthwhile from it.

Greatness wasn't worth it. Hard work to find happiness wasn't worth it. Accomplishments weren't worth it. Rewards weren't worth it. Take it from possibly the wisest man ever, striving for success isn't going to give you meaning. His life was filled with emptiness and exhaustion.

Friend, you may strive to be a success and get what you want, but you may not like what you end up with.

In James 3:16, the passage gives insight into everything that can come with high-performance and high achievements. *"For where you have envy and selfish ambition, there you find disorder and every evil practice"*. Due to your ambition to be successful and do great things it can cause more damage than you expected. While you were pressuring yourself to get the degrees, fighting for the corner office, becoming the top salesman, or getting the prized position, you found yourself hurting others, cutting corners, stepping on people, making enemies, being dishonest, and life at the top didn't make you any happier.

More success and taking the next step on the ladder won't make you feel better about yourself. The most important way to measure your worth is not to have more. The best way to measure your self-worth and significance is considering one word in every pursuit, relationship, position, and rewards. The word is *healthy*. If you can say your life is well balanced, share enjoyment and trust in your relationships with others, find pleasure in what you do, and honor the Lord with your life, you are living a healthy and happy life. That's success with much less stress.

Most of the time, arriving in a healthy place in life is more about saying no than yes.

No Is The Best Yes

Steve was a well-known rock vocalist in the city. His voice was built for rock and blues music. He was a lead singer in many rock bands stretching over two decades. His voice wailed throughout bars, clubs, festivals, and large concert venues. He embodied the rock star image. When he would leave a band, soon after another band was knocking at the door. With this scene comes so many toxic habits and behaviors. He was a heavy alcoholic and struggled with drug use. This led Steve to a divorce during this period which produced a precious baby girl, whom he neglected to visit regularly.

After a bad break up in band, Steve found himself in a season of searching. Bands hadn't pursued him yet, but it was just a matter of time. If he wanted to jump back on the stage, he could just make some calls. But this season was different.

After falling away from God and leaving the church in his teen years, Steve was invited to join a family member at church. He was willing to go and sit through the service for them and then get back to his weekend. But as Steve listened to the minister, he opened himself to the Gospel and gave his life to Christ. What a fork in the road! Could he follow Christ and not succumb to the habits and struggles of a rock star?

Since he was in between bands, Steve began to give time to helping and serving in the church. He was really enjoying who he was becoming, and the difference God was making in his life. He decided to play an instrument for the worship team and not sing; he was fearful his ego would take over and he'd become a performer. Over these months Steve was attending men's events, helping every Sunday with music, and making new friends. He made new efforts to connect with his daughter who was now a preteen. This was a great transformation to witness.

One day I overheard him say something that sparked immediate concern for me. He mentioned a popular band had reached out and wanted him to become their lead singer. After he was finished talking with the other guy, I struck up a conversation. He told me about the invitation he received from the band. It was an amazing opportunity for him to elevate his vocal career, image, and certainly his self-worth. I asked him how the phone call ended, and he said he told them "no". I carefully asked why, and he told me he didn't want everything that life came with, including how much his ego would take over and he strived for the attention.

With one simple "no", Steve left what some would call a successful life to live free from pain, addiction, debauchery, and choose the full life he now found in his relationship with God and church community. Only fearless man can have the "cajones" to tell popularity and recognition, "No thank you".

THE NEW DEFINITION

We live in a performance-driven and achievement-driven culture. They have nothing to do with who you are as a man. In America, a successful man is recognized by what a man does. God sees success quite differently. God's definition is in who you are and living the best version of you. We are not human doings, we're human beings. It's being faithful with what and who God made us to be.

If I was back in my counselor's office today, I now know the answer I would give to her question. I would confidently say, "I am successful". It's not because someone tells me so or because of a plaque on the wall that causes me to believe it. It's not based on what or how much I do. It's based on who I'm becoming as a man. Are you who you want to be? That's the direction in which you'll find true success, fulfillment, and self-worth, if it includes godly living.

It almost feels self-absorbed affirming myself as a success. I'm a success because I am faithful with who God wants and gifts me to be. In God's eyes I'm a successful pastor, no matter how big or small my church is. I'm a successful speaker, whether I have few or many speaking engagements. I'm a successful author, not because of how many books I sell or write. Most of all, I'm a successful husband and father, not based on my highs or lows. I'm successful in each of these because I'm faithful to use and grow these areas to the glory of God.

When you and I pass away, and all our earthly success is forgotten, we won't hear our Master say, "Well done, good and *successful* servant." He will only welcome us with "Well done, good and *faithful* servant".

COURAGE QUESTIONS

1. Are you known as someone who must be successful? Where did you get that from?

2. Can you have a full and complete life without gaining any accolades? How?

3. Have you been sacrificing important things due to your personal pursuits and selfish ambition? How can you prevent it?

8

LIVING LIES
INTEGRITY

-The David Struggle-

For over a week, I was watching and looking at pornography. I'm not proud to say that, and it really sucks to admit it and put it out there. I had been pastoring our church for more than 12 years and there I was, the senior pastor shamefully looking at porn. Over those several days, I would look at it when I was alone. I can't recall what caused me to take the first look that initiated the trend, but I knew how long I had been doing it. What the heck was I doing!?! I felt like a loser, was embarrassed, and didn't want anyone to find out. I was haunted by lacking in my integrity, but I didn't want to stay in this condition only for it to get increasingly worse. What did I do? I told someone about it.

I contacted a close friend and shared about it. I told him I don't know when it started, but if I don't do something I don't know when it will stop. I communicated I need to be checked on and I need to check in, so I would leave it that very day and not turn back. My friend said he admired my transparency and willingness to admit it. We put together a simple plan that day, and the rest is history.

Many say, "Well Dave, you're just weak and need to get stronger." Some think you don't "run" from a situation like this, you prove you're strong by remaining until the weakness isn't a temptation anymore. Isn't that what strong guys are supposed to do? Not really. A truly bold man can admit when he's weak and susceptible to failure and compromise on the horizon. I mean, wasn't it a brave thing for me to go to a friend and admit doing what I was ashamed of? I'm not patting myself on the back, but it would've been cowardice for me to hide in my shame because I was afraid of how I would look.

At some point you have to come to a place of humility and security as a man and just say, "I suck right now, and I'm not staying this way."

TRUTH ABOUT INTEGRITY

Integrity has been described as personal honesty in relation to your moral standards. Knowing where you're at and what you're capable of. Integrity is not perfection but its realizing when you are off track morally and need a reset to be God-honoring.

The big question which helps us to evaluate where we are is, *who are you when nobody's looking?* How do you think, talk, behave, browse, handle business, when you are alone with only you to be the judge? That's who you really are. How would you feel about your integrity in the way you treat your wife and kids if you were monitored by others? That's tough but I've had to challenge myself. What about interactions with the opposite sex, decisions with business partners, language when with the fellas, and other areas?

Integrity is a high, difficult mountain to climb, but it's worth conquering. If you want to be transparent about your integrity, it will reveal a lot about who you are and where you need to clean up.

Friend, only fearless men are willing to 'fess up, and fierce enough to initiate change. It can feel unpleasant when you're willing to confront where you're falling short and decide to do something about it. It's freeing and liberating as you gain victory.

Any time we have chosen to ignore an area we are lacking in our integrity we begin to live lies.

WHAT'S YOUR ANSWER?

Years back a friend of mine was on the phone with me, sharing an issue he was working through, and he told me he needed prayer. He asked if I would keep him in prayer, and my response was, "Of course". We got off the phone and I moved on with my day. About a week later we were face to face at church as we were touching base and he was updating me on things. Then he simply asked me, "Hey, did you pray for me?" In my mind I was like "Oh crap". I was stuck. I was frozen. It felt like time stopped as I was trying to figure out how to respond. It slipped my mind, and I didn't pray for him once in the whole entire week. I felt horrible. I certainly didn't expect him to ask about it. Who does that? I'm embarrassed to say, I considered lying and just saying "yeah". For a brief second my thought pattern was, I don't want to hurt him and, on a much smaller scale, I didn't want to appear an idiot.

I decided to share the cold truth and said, "I need to be honest; I didn't pray for you. I'm so sorry". I can't describe the pain I felt for him and then how I let a friend down at a time he needed me. I could tell he was injured by it. It was not one of my shining moments. I didn't have an excuse I only told him I didn't want to lie and said I won't do that again to him. That happened more than a decade ago and we have remained very close friends. I think, as he reflects on that call, he is assured I won't promise him anything if I can't do it.

When integrity isn't valued by us, we can lie in a second to get out of a squeeze. Most times, if we hold tight to it, integrity will require uncomfortable effort, conviction, and yes, it will be humbling. It will reveal the areas where we're vulnerable to lower our standards.

As I felt about an inch small, I asked my friend to forgive me, and he willingly did even in his hurt. I made some changes that day. Almost every time someone asks me for prayer, I tell them: "Let's pray right now." Not only does it encourage them in that moment, but my word will be kept and any other time during the week if I can pray, I will. If you ever see me on the street and ask me to pray, have a couple minutes handy so we can pray right there.

Ecclesiastes 5:7 says, *"It is better not to make a vow than to make one and not fulfill it. Do not let your mouth lead you into sin."* If we're going to be fearless men of integrity, keeping our word is where it starts. Don't commit to something if you are able, or willing, to fulfill it. I can summarize this scripture with wise words of comedian Chris Farley, "shut yer yapper". Integrity is the space between your talk and your walk. If there's a large gap, your integrity needs to be addressed.

I love what Alan Simpson, a senator from Wyoming, once said regarding integrity, "If you have integrity, nothing else matters. If you don't have integrity, nothing else matters." The notoriety of accomplishments and rewards diminish when others see we aren't what we claim to be.

How would people – *who really know you* – describe your integrity?

THE ALTER EGO

The epic story of a boy becoming king is iconic. Even people who aren't Christians are aware of the biblical hero, David. He was the shepherd boy who slayed the giant Goliath with a stone and his sling shot, who was then celebrated and honored as a great warrior in the history of Israel. He would be anointed to become the next, and most famous, king. What an incredible man.

But there are some portions of his life less popular and less heroic. They're not pretty and tear away at the reputation of David. His morality and godliness are left in shambles after he makes decisions which violate his integrity.

This story is a familiar one, which ends in disaster due to King David's alter ego. Though he should have been joining his army in battle, from his rooftop, David notices his attractive neighbor, Bathsheba, washing. He sends his men to take her back to the palace, he has sex with her, and she conceives. To cover up the pregnancy, David recalls Bathsheba's husband Uriah from the siege of Rabbah, so he would have sex with his wife to appear Uriah was the one who impregnated her. But Uriah has too much integrity to sleep with his wife while the rest of the army and the ark are camping in tents. David tries two times, along with trying to get him drunk, to get Uriah to compromise and to be with her. Since

David couldn't get Uriah to give up his integrity, he conspires with Joab, the commander of the army, by orchestrating Uriah's death in battle as Joab put him on the front lines. David assumes the disaster has been averted. But David doesn't take God into account.

He has developed an alter ego, a different version of himself, a lie. It is a life of gratification and compromises that strokes his personal ego. There's an acrostic for the word EGO, which is Edging God Out. This is precisely what David did as he made a series of decisions focusing on himself while neglecting God and ignoring others. He significantly damaged his integrity.

Here are some steps in David's story that are common with us men as well. It's important to take note of these so we can learn from him and correct our own.

David reduced the importance of God's expectations

"In the spring of the year, when kings normally go out to war, David sent Joab and the Israelite army to fight..." (2 Samuel 11:1, NLT).

The Lord gave David an incredible opportunity to lead God's people, which of course came with "normal" responsibility. As we all know, *"To whom much is given, much will be required"*. As David assumes this role, it comes with the standards and duties of kingship. He is required to fulfill the standard of the King of Israel. But, at some point he takes a break from it, and this is not suitable for one who seeks to honor God. This would become his first and foundational mistake.

When we reduce the expectations of the Lord as options we can take a break from, it is dishonoring to God. We have given his standards less importance in our lives. God's heavenly expectations are to be number one in the life of a godly man. When we read them in scripture, they are to be our highest goal. We cannot manufacture our own or copy how others may honor God's word. Our measuring stick is God's word. Are God's expectations the most important goals in your life?

Integrity isn't half-way, or conditional. It's all or none.

David enjoyed his own comfort and pleasure

"One late afternoon, David got up from taking his nap and was strolling on the roof of the palace." (2 Samuel 11:2, MSG).

David is now lowering his guard and allowing his fleshly desires to grab his attention. He is taking a "nap" on the job and "strolling" as he glances at his kingdom, unintentionally finding himself engaged and filled with lust. His own comfort and pleasure become a tool of the enemy to destroy this man's great reputation he once had.

He wasn't alert or marching as he would be in battle but has been given permission to sin by enjoying his luxuries. Thus, his integrity is compromised, and he pursues the unthinkable. His idle time would prove to be destructive.

David surrounded himself with the wrong people

"From his vantage point on the roof he saw a woman bathing. The woman was stunningly beautiful. David sent to ask about her, and was told, 'Isn't this Bathsheba, daughter of Eliam and wife of Uriah the Hittite?' David sent his agents to get her. After she arrived, he went to bed with her." (2 Samuel 11:2-4, MSG).

Though it wasn't Bathsheba's fault David had the "vantage point" of her body, and lust was conceived, he allowed her beauty to be an object of sin. Then he has agents to fetch her for himself instead of guarding or having any regard for his integrity, and most importantly, her dignity.

Beware of the influences you allow in your life. The company you keep will impact your goal to honor God with your thoughts, behavior, and actions. Who is in your life that doesn't prioritize godly character? You and I reflect the friendships we keep. David "went to bed with her" out of his own doing. True, godly men won't open you to sinful living and certainly won't permit you to go that direction without saying something.

David deceived others by covering up his secrets

"Then David said to Uriah, 'Go home. Have a refreshing bath and a good night's rest.' After Uriah left the palace… David wrote a letter to Joab and sent it with Uriah. In the letter he wrote, 'Put Uriah in the front lines where the fighting is the fiercest. Then pull back and leave him exposed so that he's sure to be killed.'" (2 Samuel 11:8, 14-15, MSG).

David has not only committed sexual sin. By this point he is deceitful and malicious. His life is becoming a lie. He even goes a step further and orders a man to be murdered.

When you and I sin, and leave it unconfessed, it will multiply. Usually, our first response is to cover up and hide what we've done. If you find yourself needing to hide something, you're hiding sin in your life and compartmentalizing your public persona and private pleasures.

David offended people around him

"So Joab, holding the city under siege, put Uriah in a place where he knew there were fierce enemy fighters. When the city's defenders came out to fight Joab, some of David's soldiers were killed, including Uriah." (2 Samuel 11:16-17, MSG).

David is leading Joab to sin and conspire with him to take someone's life. What selfish behavior we possess when we don't recognize how we will hurt others around us.

Your sin, my sin, will find us out…and others will find out too. Many men take the approach of "it's my life", though their lives are emotionally attached to others. We can cause painful offense to those closest to us. And guess whose responsibility it is…ours.

If you're Joab, Bathsheba or one of David's agents, you've closely watched this man, king, warrior, and someone they respected do all he did, how can you trust him? If he'll go to these lengths with others, why won't he do the same with you or to you? I'm sure they found themselves to some degree losing trust in him.

TRUST LEVELS

Our personal integrity, good or bad, will determine the trust in the relationships we have with others. Our integrity levels determine trust levels. People can be certain to know who you are, or have reservations, regarding your reactions and/or pro-actions. You become a questionable individual if you are flippant with your integrity.

In James 1:8 (AMP), James, the brother says, *"A man of two minds (irresolute), [he is] unstable and unreliable and uncertain about everything [he thinks, feels, decides]."*

Thoughts and feelings of a double-minded man cause him to teeter on the hinge of convenience and conditions benefiting himself. None of us have planned to be an unstable, unreliable, or an uncertain person.

Yet it is common for men to be upset with people when they don't fully trust them. When wives, children, coworkers, and supervisors don't believe them or ask for their help they become frustrated. Somewhere along the way they have done something that makes them unstable, unreliable, or uncertain. Have you found yourself feeling this way with individuals? Ask yourself, "what have I done?"

Once you identify it you can make the necessary plans to correct and restore your integrity.

This begs the questions, are you the same in all places, at all times, with all people? Are you trustworthy in every area of your life?

Your integrity will be easily evaluated by the consistency and depth others are willing to trust you.

UNAPOLOGETIC INTEGRITY

I was talking to a guy who occasionally took business trips for his job. He was happily married with children. I respected him as a man of integrity. He shared with me a point when his integrity was tested and his reputation was on the line.

On one trip, as he checked in to the hotel where he was staying, a nice, pretty lady at the concierge was checking him in. They were having small, typical conversation as this was happening. During the conversation she was taking a liking to him, he would later realize, and began to flirt though his wedding ring was noticeably on his ring finger. As she finished the paperwork and gave him the key to his room, it was clear she knew he was traveling alone. When he was about to walk away, she asked, "What are you doing tonight?" He was caught off guard. She then asked if he wanted to go out that night, even though he was married. He was paralyzed by the bluntness of this seductive lady. I loved the response he transparently told me. He said to her, "I gotta go!" as he turned his back and took off.

He made no apologies for his strict integrity. That was awesome! You don't have to be polite when temptation is threatening your godliness. Just run. Take off. Fearless men don't care what people think or how they'll be talked about. They won't give the enemy any room ensnare them.

LOYALTY TO GOD

Even though David had major collapses at times, in 1 Samuel 13:14 the Lord said of David's life, *"I have found David son of Jesse a man after my own heart; he will do everything I want him to do."* God never declared him to be perfect but knew ultimately David would continue to turn to God in all things.

If we want to be men of integrity, we can practice some of the things David wrote in scripture which reflected the heart of a man who was loyal to God's desires. Here are three things you and I can do on a daily basis to strengthen, maintain, and/or repair integrity as we live out God's moral standards.

Integrity Check in

In this psalm David gets courageously vulnerable and opens himself to the Lord for correction in his integrity. *"Search me, O God, and know my heart; test me and know my anxious thoughts. Point out anything in me that offends you, and lead me along the path of everlasting life."* (Psalm 139:23-24, NLT).

It's a bold thing to sit before the Lord and ask him to expose anything that offends him which are residing in your heart and mind for. When we take this daring step, the Holy Spirit will caringly convict you and we have an opportunity to admit our guilt. It's for the simple reason to be aware of the areas needing correction.

The Spirit strengthens our integrity when we choose to check in every part of us.

Integrity Clean Up

It's not enough to just know about what we've done, but we must ask the Spirit to clean out the corruption it has caused in our souls. Here David is yearning to be pure, holy, and clean before God. *"Create in me a new, clean heart, O God, filled with clean thoughts and right desires."* (Psalm 51:10, TLB). Some think the job is over when they find relief from repenting, but action must follow.

The Spirit repairs our integrity when we choose to clean up our hearts and minds as we move forward.

Integrity Carry Out

New days are ahead when we have decided to be vulnerable with God and be cleansed in our hearts. We begin to strive for progress. David details his spiritual growth plan in this passage. *"Your word is a lamp to my feet and a light for my path."* (Psalm 119:105, NIV).

David relied on the word of God to grow and maintain healthy integrity and loyalty to God. The Bible is God's primary way of speaking to us. When we are reading the Bible, he will help us carry out his will and honor him.

The Spirit maintains our integrity when we choose to carry out His divine commands.

Fearless men continually work on their integrity.

?

COURAGE QUESTIONS

1. With all honesty, do you believe others see you as a person of integrity? Why?

2. What is something you do in private, which compromises your integrity, that conflicts with who you are in public?

3. What's an area in your life you must stop compartmentalizing and establish more integrity? How will you begin?

9

DIRTY DEEDS
PURITY

- The Samson Struggle –

I still remember my first-time watching pornography at the innocent age of seven in a room with 13-year-old boys.

Before that day I had never even heard of this material. If I try to, even today as a middle-aged man, I can still recall portions of that video I stored up when my second-grade mind was contaminated by the view of sexual perversion. That's when the first seeds of dirty deeds, sexual immorality, were sewn. They would multiply over my younger years and become my life-journey of fighting for purity, in my mind, in my body, and through my eyes.

Over my years, as I matured into manhood, sexual immorality increased in dark ways…in some ways that are common to men. We can engage in more porn, masturbation, promiscuity, undress women in our minds (for some maybe its men), sexually perverted talk, attend strip clubs, watch "soft" porn, and more. It sounds dirty, but if all were fully transparent, I believe every man has acted on more than one of these behaviors, easily.

I remember talking to a man about how he wrestled with some of these same things, and he said he thought this drive would go away when he got older; he was almost 60. By the way single guy, the drive doesn't disappear when you're married just because you have God's permission and freedom to have sex as frequent as you desire with your wife.

An older minister I know and admire has openly stated to his church that all his life he's had an attraction to porn. He guards himself against it because he sure does like it if he begins to look at it. I'm convinced most of us can agree.

In this chapter I won't dance around or hint at things because it can be an uncomfortable topic. You may even feel it's too graphic. This chapter is hope-filled for some and a warning for others. This is too much of a issue in our culture to skirt around the dirty stuff. It threatens the health of your closest relationships. I want to normalize this conversation so all men can come out of hiding and feel safe to discuss their struggles. If you want to fight the struggle and live in purity you must know how bad it is and can become.

Let me give you some hope. You can get out of any sexual sin controlling you and have victory. We all can.

ENSLAVED TO SEX

Adrian's sex addiction began early in his teens. He was exposed to pornography in his pre-teen years, which helped create an intense sexual appetite. This was way before porn was just a click away. In those times you had to search for it, find friends who had it, or older men who could buy it in the local convenience stores for you. Due to viewing graphic content, masturbation became habitual. He then began to have relationships with girls, which were based on him viewing them as sexual objects to conquest. Many of the girls he was having sex were from his own church youth group. These experiences became numerous and regular with different girls over time. This would only gain momentum.

Adrian was faithful in his church and youth group, having high hopes of one day going into ministry God was calling him to. He hoped prayer would make this craving go away, but he only experienced greater grief and guilt he would carry for years.

Sadly, Adrian's sex addiction was the fruit of painful childhood experiences. Beginning at the age of seven years old, he encountered sexual abuse from a foster child living in his home. He had no clue what was happening other than a good feeling sensation that he innocently enjoyed. This abuse would continue until he was 12 years old, which during that time another boy would end up abusing him as well. It was at that age while masturbating he climaxed for the first time, which opened a new world of sexual pleasure. A world he would find himself enslaved to.

Going into his twenties, Adrian would go through seasons of not having sex with girls, and struggled with clearing his mind of strong desires to have more sex or be exposed to it. This weighed heavy on him. It was a private struggle that haunted him, and he never considered telling someone who could help, fearing he would be shamed and/or punished. He discovered a part-time ministry he could be involved in, but still carried this excruciating burden he couldn't escape. He found himself reconnecting with girls for sex over periods of time while committed in this ministry experience. He would watch movies which had sexual content, and thus masturbation had become a daily lifestyle. One night he was driving in the city and found himself in the red-light district, pulled over on the side of the road soliciting a prostitute. Midway through the conversation a godly fear rushed over him, and he awoke from this controlling lustful encounter and sped away, shocked by how low he had stooped during this painful battle of sexual addiction and sin.

Adrian finally realized he couldn't break this stronghold alone; he grew desperate and asked for help. He brought godly, caring men into his life who were focused on setting him free, not condemning him. Today, following decades of efforts of discipline to maintain the freedom from the burden of lust, he now helps other men break free from their sexual addictions.

The Cleveland Clinic defines sex addiction as *"excessive sexual thoughts, desires, urges or behaviors that can't be controlled and cause distress and harm to your relationships, finances, and other aspects of your life. Sexual addiction is also called hypersexuality,* compulsive sexual behavior *and other names."*

It is not just a drive to have sex regularly. It's just like a drug addict gets his daily fix first thing in the morning and throughout the day, spending his time consumed with the next fix, scrambling for money, and carelessly overlooks responsibilities. The same daily pattern applies to the sex addict. All the while, for many Christian men, wait for the pain of guilt to accompany this sex addiction as it continues to master them.

Adrian had a sex addiction which took him places he never anticipated. But through God's power, he was delivered, and now lives free from the controlling power of lust and shame.

SEXUAL SUFFERING

Many years ago, I sat in on a group discussion with some good Christian guys. Their goal in this intensive was to grow in godliness, focusing mainly on their sexuality.

One man chose to take a turn sharing what he was going through and had struggled with for years. It was a private anguish and very difficult to discuss. You could tell it haunted him and he was a wreck inwardly.

He was a successful businessman which called for him to travel nationally to many cities on a weekly basis. The cities he visited were regions of which he gave oversight. He had been in this industry for years and traveled as his family was at home during each week. By the time he shared this, he was middle-aged, had been married for decades and his kids were grown-up, some with their own children. He and his wife raised them in a good Christian home and regularly attended church over the years. But he had a secret that literally no one, not one person, knew the secret eating at his soul like acid.

Each time he visited a city there were men he was familiar with, not necessarily friends, which he would meet up for sexual encounters. There were several men, in several cities, for several years. As he shared, you could feel the deep brokenness of a man who could not stop meeting with men as he had a longing to be loved by a man. It wasn't an erotic love he craved, but a caring love, which expressed itself in a lustful way.

He had a painful upbringing, which included being molested by an extended male family member, and the relationship with his father was distant, which hurt him most because he felt he wasn't a "real" boy. Out of his brokenness he longed for a masculine love his wife couldn't give but needed it from his father. The wounds he carried were too much to bear. You could tell this man desperately wanted to escape the prison of living lies almost all his life. His wife nor children knew. His life would end up in shambles if he ever revealed the dark, secret struggle that controlled him.

He was filled with shame due to his sexual appetite, guilt over the homosexual sin he was constantly reminded of, and hopelessness believing he could never find victory. What a brave decision he made choosing not to fight alone. He was beginning to take steps toward a victorious journey.

WANTING BUT UNWANTED

After spending so many hours helping men one-on-one or in groups, I've discovered a fresh perspective I think will give relief to all men regarding sexual sin, lust, and sexuality that doesn't conform to God's word. I'm convinced sexual sin is not wanted in us men who have chosen to live sexually pure. I've seen men bogged down, defeated, and feel helpless with these.

The perspective I've taken on for myself, and what I encourage men to take on when their sexuality is ungodly, is accepting you have an "*unwanted sexual desire*" in whatever form it may be. What I mean is, in our fleshly nature we like and enjoy sexual immorality in its various forms. You may ask, "How can you say that, Dave?" Because we wouldn't struggle with purity if we only had God-honoring sexual thoughts and behaviors.

Deep down we don't want the sexual struggle we keep fighting. Though you like it, you don't want it, but you like it, but you don't want it, and so on. How do you get rid of something that's pleasurable yet makes you miserable simultaneously? When we have finally had a clear moment of truth with ourselves, we become resolute with mindsets such as, "I hate this, I don't want it, it's controlling me, and I'm not living this way anymore."

Freedom is potentially on the horizon…unless you choose to enjoy the sexual sin and don't believe it's affecting your life.

THE TOUGH, ARROGANT, IGNORANT, WEAKING

You may have heard of Samson before. He was a man God created to be ferociously strong and God gave him supernatural power unknown to mankind, and that's not an exaggeration. There were a few qualifiers which Samson needed to honor until the day he died to maintain this gift from God. He had a special Nazirite covenant, which meant he wasn't allowed to eat forbidden animals according to Mosaic law, drink alcohol, or cut his hair. If he maintained this covenant, the strength he had would be with him for God's use to accomplish his will. It wasn't at his personal disposal to use for his own desires.

The feats and exploits of Samson's rare encounters are documented in scripture. Gaza was one of the five major cities of the Philistines, with city gates believed to be approximately 10ft x10ft. Samson removed and took not only the gates but the connected posts as well. One estimate is that the gates weighed between five and 10 tons. He then carried them for some 40 miles, uphill. He tore a lion apart with his bare hands. He captured 300 foxes, lit their tales on fire, and turned them loose to burn fields. In one incident he took a jawbone of a donkey and slayed 1,000 Philistines all by himself. These are just a few of the supernatural things he accomplished when the Spirit of God rushed upon him.

Unfortunately, Samson would end up violating the Nazirite covenant and, to add injury to insult, he would openly pursue a sexually immoral life. Sexual immorality refers to any sexual activity outside of the morals God established when He created it for intimacy with wives only. Outside of this, sex is twisted for one's own pleasure and gratification.

Mostly this journey is a gradual slide not a deliberate action. If we choose to entertain our human sexual desires, over time we take our eyes off God and His design for good and healthy sexuality. We see right out of the gate Samson is full of "self", concerned only with "self", and consumed with pleasing "self".

> *"Samson went down to Timnah, and at Timnah he saw one of the daughters of the Philistines. Then, he came up and told his father and mother, "I saw one of the daughters of the Philistines at Timnah. Now get her for me as my wife." But his father and mother said to him, "Is there not a woman...among all our people, that you must go to take a wife from the uncircumcised Philistines?" But Samson said to his father, "Get her for me, for she is right in my eyes." Judges 14:1-3 (ESV)*

Timnah was a city Philistines took away from Judah, a rival people of Israel. In Hebrew Timnah means *"Forbidden"*. Could it be any clearer for Samson he is headed for trouble? By name the city was a message to him, it's not yours to have. Sadly, this is a journey we as men take when we opt to flirt with something when we have no business entertaining. The behavior described in these passages become a way of life for Samson as he continually repeats this pattern. It is a pattern focused on "self" which can be defined in four phases of this selfish cycle.

Self-Gratification

"He saw one of the daughters of the Philistines." Samson demanded to have this woman for himself. He would pressure his parents to arrange a marriage with her. It was based on what he "saw". He didn't get to know her or go on any dates. She simply became an object to bring pleasure to himself. If we can agree, it probably wasn't "one look". It was more than one which probably led to inappropriate, and lust-filled thoughts. It may have started with the initial excuse of the average man, "It won't hurt to look." The more you and I flirt with "only looking" it will end up hurting us as we allow gratification to replace conviction.

Self-Entitlement

Two times Samson tells his parents, *"Get her for me"*. Now I don't know how or when he became comfortable bossing his parents around. Apparently, they were used to this behavior. It's obvious as his urges increased his mind was made up, "if I want her, I can have her". No one could tell him differently. Our lust can take over us like it did for him. If I have to sneak, if it causes conflict, if it goes against God's Word, it is not mine for the taking.

Self-Serving

His parents pled with him to take the correct and God-honoring route. They compelled him to take a wife *"among our people."* It didn't matter how it affected anyone else, Samson was willing to mortgage his future and legacy to embrace a forbidden craving. How many times have we lost sight of what's right long-term and trade it for temporary enjoyment? We choose to serve our uncontrolled urges and eventually those same urges now control us. At one point we crossed the threshold of, "I'm gonna do me."

Self-Deception

It has become a very common thread in our culture today for people to "live your truth." The problem with this belief is, if you replace God's truth to create your own your life, it is all about your "self". Whose truth will you hold to? Samson follows his "truth" when he finally states, *"she is right in my eyes."* Seeing life through the eyes of the Lord takes the backseat. What you feel and want are now your guiding truth. The lie we tell ourselves is, "if it is right in my eyes then its ok, and no one can argue with it". So, we override God's definition of sex as he created.

My friend, if you plan to live a godly life, the only truth for your sexuality is what God has spoken through the Bible.

For all of us godly men we must hold tight to the belief that, *my sexuality doesn't belong to me*. When we come to Christ and surrender all, we no longer have ownership of our money, ambitions, and yes, also our sex life. My sexual identity isn't mine and my standard for purity isn't up for debate. He didn't make a mistake when creating each of us or give us permission to come up with their own. *The sex life God permits comes with no worries, no disease, no surprises, no regrets, no controversies, no pain, and no problems.* Sexual intimacy designed by God, between one biological man and one biological woman within legally recognized marriage, is void of all these complications.

ILLICIT SEX

Samson continues down a road of depravity in his life which even involves soliciting a prostitute. He also ends up marrying another "forbidden" Philistine woman due to illicit sexuality for a man of God, sex that is prohibited and not permitted. When we follow this type of lifestyle and illicit habits, it will come with a cost as it did in the end as Samson discovered. Like the Philistines were preparing a trap for him, Satan is using sexual immorality and lust as a trap for us. This is what transpired for Samson as he never gained control.

> *"He loved a woman in the Valley of Sorek, whose name was Delilah. And the lords of the Philistines came up to her and said to her, "Seduce him, and see where his great strength lies, and by what means we may overpower him, that we may bind him to humble him". (Judges 16:4-5, ESV).*

The scriptures start with Samson *"loved"*. This is not a caring, committed, or kind love he has for this foreign woman. The word love in this context comes from the Hebrew word *ahabb,* referring to an erotic sexual attraction. The word is closely related to an Arabic word meaning *"to breathe hard"* or *"to be excited"*. He continually proved to be enslaved by physical sensuality.

Delilah was pressured to use this as a weakness to conquer Samson and destroy him. What she ends up doing to him is precisely what we experience when we participate in sexual behavior, whether alone or with someone, which is illicit in the eyes of God. Our drive and appetite lead us down a road where we are overpowered and bound because our purity defenses weren't in operation.

Our greatest defense, and offense, is sexual purity. A sex life free of perversion. Remember this, *pursuing purity prevents perversion.*

When we choose biblical sexuality, we circumvent these perverted experiences by pursuing purity. The drive towards purity helps us to implement boundaries to prevent hurt and damage in our lives. Remember when it comes to boundaries, there is freedom within boundaries. You have freedom in your spirit because you are not bound or corrupted in your sexuality.

If only Samson made this his pursuit, he would have less likely lost his strength, been captured, or had his eyes gouged out. What is most grievous is how his Nazirite covenant was completely violated and the Spirit of God no longer held this place in his life. He found this out the hard and shocking way when Judges 16:20 states, *"he did not know that the LORD had left him"*. He lost everything. That's typically what illicit sex results in, you lose…big.

If we're going to avoid seduction, being overpowered, and bound in our sexuality we must understand what the perversion consists of so we can overcome each of them with purity. They're uncomfortable and uncommon to discuss among men but absolutely vital, firstly in your relationship with God.

Over the years of giving pastoral counseling to men and couples, these seeds of corruption come to the surface and need to be addressed. I'm not generating these, but they have been questioned by people who really want to know what is right and what is wrong. Most understand pornography is sinful because it is objectifying the sex of other people for your own stimulation. Masturbation is wrong because giving oneself physical pleasure while entertaining sinful lust and covetousness (remember sex is between a man and a woman not even alone). Bisexuality, homosexuality, and transsexuality are wrong because they violate the design of sex between one man and one woman in marriage. People have asked about threesomes, either including a third person in their intimacy or entertaining pornography together…along with these, sexual jokes, connotations, or conversations are also impure. They're all off limits for godly men.

TEMPLE DETOX

Our bodies must be habitually detoxed of every bit of immorality in us. If you want Holy Spirit power moving in your life you are the only one who can prevent sexual sin. One of the best ways to maintain this healthy perspective is giving thoughtful implementation of the words in 1 Corinthians 6:19-20. *"Do you not know that your body is a temple of the Holy Spirit, who is in you, whom you have received from God? You are not your own; you were bought at a price. Therefore, honor God with your body."*

What an illustration given for us to comprehend the sacredness and holiness we must aspire to maintain in our bodies. Our highest goal sexually is to honor God with our bodies. Apostle Paul relates your body to a temple or church or sanctuary, helping us grasp how pure we must aspire to be. Anything unholy, perverted, or immoral must be removed from the premises without compromise or excuses.

As we accept Paul's concept of our bodies to be like sanctuaries in a church, consider the corruption of sexual sin is unfit in the sexuality of a man. It's graphic, not to be sensational, but to raise our understanding of holiness and perversion. Would you ever masturbate or look at pornography sitting in a church pew? Would you ever fornicate or commit adultery there? How about "hooking up" with someone you met on the internet? Would you openly tell dirty jokes full of sexual connotations with others sitting in your row? This is serious. How could the Holy Spirit ever move supernaturally amidst this behavior? We can't expect God to flow through our life while living immorally. Your spiritual life is on the line. It requires a fierce, intentional, and fearless plan to live in purity. Purity will become your pathway to sexual freedom.

I strongly recommend your wife is *not* part of your purity pursuit. Most times, they cannot handle the reality of our struggle, nor can they absorb the blow when you have a setback. Since women are not the visual beings we are, they can easily dismiss sexual things we can't, thus leading them to frustration. They take it personal because "you can stop if you want to, but you won't". I've heard wives say that to their husbands a handful of times. What works best is to begin changes without making promises or commitments to them. Just start doing it.

PICK THE FIGHT

Sexual immorality is not defeated by trying to abstain from it but fighting for purity. Here are some "helps" for you to initiate your fight for your purity.

- Make a covenant with the Holy Spirit to live in sexual purity.
- Begin each day consecrating over your eyes, ears, hands, and private parts through prayer.
- Stay away from locations, entertainment, and people who contribute to immorality and impurity.
- Identify common situations of temptation. (Hotels, late nights, time alone, internet, coworker, etc).
- Regularly meet with a trusted friend about your struggle for accountability, prayer, and support to keep the covenant you made with the Holy Spirit.

(Do not invite someone for accountability who possesses the same struggle).

- Seek professional counseling for healing and habits. This will help to explore and discover what your sexual addictions are rooted in. I love meeting with gifted, Christian counselors so I can be a better man. Crazy people don't go to counseling, wise people do.
- Acquire an internet service that provides accountability for everything you watch, see, and visit.
- Join a recovery program to overcome addiction.

Prepare yourself. In various ways, this more than likely be the biggest and most difficult lifelong fight you'll ever have. Be ready to fight for your purity for a lifetime not only a season.

Fearless men are willing to surrender their sexuality to God and pursue a life of freedom and purity.

?

COURAGE QUESTION

1. What is your greatest sexual temptation? Explain.

2. In what times, places, and/or with whom, are you weak and likely to commit sexual sin? Why?

3. Are you willing to establish hard boundaries to fight for your purity? Why or why not?

GROW SOME
ACCOUNTABILITY

- The Adam Struggle –

"Shut up".

That was the blunt advice he gave me when we were on the phone. He was a friend and mentor I pursued to help me grow as a young minister. I was eager to grow and learn how to conduct myself and create habits to help me sharpen my ability to care for and lead people. He had a wealth of knowledge and experience I desired to glean from. We met monthly over coffee or lunch and talked ministry and leadership. I'd come with questions about things I was curious about, and he would share all he knew. He showed his belief in me and it meant a lot to me. I didn't want someone to tell me things I wanted to hear but also things I needed to hear. I wasn't looking for someone to agree with me while I make mistakes. There was one reason I enjoyed having this close, confident relationship is that I could share my struggles, difficulties, and get help when I might harm my growth as a minister.

One year I was having a challenging stint with the pastor in the church I worked. There was tension developing within me. I was growing impatient in my position and had thoughts I wanted to express to the pastor. I shared all of this with my mentor on the phone one day in an irritated state. I didn't want to screw anything up, but I didn't want things to stay the same. After explaining everything I asked my mentor what I should say or do. His response was, "Dave you just need to shut up and not say anything". It was direct and came from a place of love.

I welcomed it and did as he advised me to…and I'm grateful to this day. I had someone who cared enough to challenge me and hold me accountable so I could reach my full potential.

SERVE OR BE SERVED

Accountability is an interesting dynamic. We have the choice to defer accountability for our actions and decisions, or we can opt for accountability as a guide to minimize regretful behaviors. Accountability is when we are subjected to explain, answer for, or take responsibility for things we have done. If we decide to subject ourselves to accountability in advance, we are inviting wisdom to help guide us and make corrections towards a fruitful life with less harm. We can also decide to live and behave the way we want and simply be responsible for it later. Sadly, most men take the latter course, causing harm, making constant mistakes, and will have to answer for all of it in the end.

Most men are afraid to acquire accountability, challenged to live up to a godly standard, into their lives because they'd rather blame someone, or they feel threatened they'll lose freedom, or be condemned.

The late author Bob Proctor said, "Accountability is the glue that ties commitment to results". If you want to be the very best godly version of you, accountability is your advocate. Men who are willing to "grow some stones" and have someone else watch after them out of care and concern, will see the most fruit living as a godly man. Only fearless men will invest time to find someone to hold them accountable and follow through with it.

Many men shrug off inviting accountability into their lives because the transparency it demands will reveal areas that are incorrect, deficient, weak, or ashamed of. These are usually the people saying common phrases like, "Only God can judge me", or "God knows my heart". These are the words of those who don't want to be held responsible for change or correction. These are the excuses of those running from accountability. And by the way, God will judge. He does know our hearts, and the reason we chose those answers as a response.

When we choose to live with transparency, that comes with accountability, we remove the power of secrets restricting us from godly standard of living the Lord desires. No one can make you have accountability in your life, but it will bring credibility to your reputation. You must open your life and initiate it.

THE SHIFT

Adam, the first man in the Bible, did everything but take responsibility or own his failure. He certainly didn't have accountability that would position himself for success.

God initially told Adam, he and Eve can have anything in all creation to themselves, but not the tree of knowledge of good and evil. The first sin in the Bible occurs in Genesis when the devil, disguised as a serpent, deceives Eve her into eating this fruit along with Adam that resulted in God's judgment.

Genesis 3:4-6, 9-12, 17

> *"You will not surely die," the serpent said to the woman. "For God knows that when you eat of it your eyes will be opened, and you will be like God, knowing good and evil." When the woman saw that the fruit of the tree was good for food and pleasing to the eye, and also desirable for gaining wisdom, she took some and ate it. She also gave some to her husband, who was with her, and he ate it...the LORD God called to the man, "Where are you?" He answered, "I heard you in the garden, and I was afraid because I was naked; so I hid." And he said, "Who told you that you were naked? Have you eaten from the tree that I commanded you not to eat from?" The man said, "The woman **you** put here with me—she gave me some fruit from the tree, and I ate it."... To Adam he said, "Because you listened to your wife and ate from the tree about which I commanded you, 'You must not eat*

119

of it,' "Cursed is the ground because of you; through painful toil you will eat of it all the days of your life."

Adam wouldn't take responsibility and be held accountable. As a matter of fact, in his mind it's God's fault and Eve's responsibility for this happening. When we put off defining our preferred destiny, we live aimlessly with a trail of unnecessary consequences. Why not avoid as many as possible? Choosing the way of accountability is pre-deciding what your desired outcome of your life will be. Undecidedness results in an uncertain future for you, this is the chasm men typically never cross. What area do you need to decide you must have accountability for? Might it be to strengthen your Christian testimony, improve your fathering, stop mistreating your wife, gain financial wisdom, maintain sexual purity, hold a job, stop lying and deceiving, flirting or inappropriate relationships with other women? Your life can be incredibly fulfilling, you decide.

THE SWEET EMBRACE

Committing to accountability positions you for success if you're willing to embrace the following mentalities. These are intimidating steps for many men because they identify accountability with punishment or condemnation. It's more about positioning yourself for success. Only men who choose to grow some stones possess the courage to discover the blessing of accountability. It's something to embrace in your life and not tolerate.

Here are three ways to benefit from accountability.

Confess to your accountability partner to enable growth

As I read this story I wonder, what if Adam and Eve shared accountability between the two of them? I mean, they saw the fruit was "Good and pleasing", it was enticing. If they kept checking and confessing when they were tempted, they would've had a better chance of not succumbing to the enemy's temptations. Confession of weaknesses and failures enables us to see where growth is needed and how to have it.

120

I had a conversation with a man who was in his early twenties and running into challenges at work. He wasn't the best at self-discipline and completing tasks and this would bring about difficult conversations with employers. He had a desire to be liked and please people so, when he was questioned regarding unfinished work, he would lie to get around feeling bad and letting someone down. Since he wasn't forthright this only made employment increasingly difficult to maintain over the years. When he'd find himself in these situations, he'd either get away with lying or just quit before the truth was found out. He avoided the blessing of accountability. He couldn't simply confess this to a mentor and then find opportunities to grow and experience character transformation. A man with this type of character will suffer until he finally acknowledges and confesses, he has a problem and wants to do something about it.

Here is a major point to remember, a man who admits mistakes and failures can be trusted in the long run if they pursue growth. We all have defaults, what will you do to overcome them?

Long ago I decided I longed for accountability so I could mature and grow. I was willing to "tell on myself" to get on the fast track to success.

Submit to your accountability partner to make corrections

Along with the devil playing a part in his sinful decision, Adam blames God then Eve for what transpired when he says, "the woman you put here with me---she gave me some". It's a little humorous to read what he actually told God.

Trent struggled with alcohol addiction for years. In some seasons he drank whenever he was awake, maintaining a buzz, and sometimes would stop for a period of time only to go on drunken binges. We had set up some agreed boundaries, most of which he suggested. He submitted to the commitment and the accountability of answering for what he'd failed in, or what we could celebrate.

Trent would do well but when he fell off and went on binges his response was to blame his wife and the friends who would buddy up and go to bars with him. He'd mention how she would drink, so he would. Or she made their relationship toxic and "drove him" to drink. He couldn't submit to calling some men who supported him in these times or do what he was lovingly directed to do so he wouldn't fail. As long as he blamed, he couldn't make any corrections.

Robert Anthony, a professor at Harvard Business School, once stated: "When you blame others you give up your power to change". Trent continuously gave up power to change.

Men who blame shift and don't submit to those who care, won't advance in life because they refuse to see their wrong and won't improve.

Depend on your accountability partner for guidance to finish well

We have a benefit Adam didn't have in his arsenal. We have men we can turn to and have accountability when we are encouraged by various to do what we're trying to avoid. When Eve was the only voice speaking to him, he was tempted to take the fruit, and found himself powerless to give in. He didn't have anyone else to turn to.

We not only have people we can bring into our lives for accountability, but it's vital we're realistic about times we're weak and tempted. Many men tend to feel they need to be strong in these times and defeat the onslaught coming at them, only to see they were limited. At times we are powerless because we are facing areas of weakness. Don't try to muscle up, think you're strong enough, and believe it's a test to prove it. Why put pressure to be strong when you have reinforcements to ensure you finish well?

Chase is now a very successful businessman and God is really blessing his efforts. But early in his mid-twenties, Chase made a severely poor decision which resulted in a tragic ending. One late evening he and some friends visited a nightclub for some dancing, social time, and drinking hard liquor. As it grew close to closing time, they headed outside to the parking lot and prepared to go home. Chase was elected to drive because he seemed to be mostly sober. As Chase was driving down the highway, still intoxicated, he lost control of the steering wheel and the car ended up flipping several times to an horrific stop. It was a fatal accident where one of his friends lost his life. On top of the heavy and unshakable guilt Chase carried, he was eventually convicted of involuntary vehicular manslaughter. Instead of finishing his education at a prominent university, he would spend over three years in state penitentiary.

Recognizing that accountability from other men could have prevented this deadly occurrence is a hard pill of regret to swallow. If you and I don't embrace accountability as a treasured friend, we will be held responsible for any foolish decisions, or indecisions, we make. There will be penalties – whether its minor regrets or major pain.

Adam and Eve were talked into giving into their temptation in a time of weakness, and so was

Chase. What they really needed was someone to talk them out of it. Chase could have been positioned for success from one phone call, an Uber, or text for wise advice. But instead, he was doomed for failure and only he was responsible for it. If he had accountability he could have depended on a mentor and finished that night on a good note.

You and I have the power to decide if we will finish well. Will we depend only on ourselves in our weak times, or depend on those who are stronger in those moments? Surround yourself with godly guidance.

THE GRIND THAT TRIES US

This scripture is a catchy phrase many churches and Christian men name their ministries. It is also used as a theme for special events. It's a powerful and encouraging statement, but it's not necessarily a pretty picture or comfortable process like we imagine. Proverbs 27:17 (NLT): *"As iron sharpens iron, so a friend sharpens a friend"*.

The beginning of friction between two raw pieces of iron isn't comfortable, but the end is. As you and I commit to a relationship that challenges our godliness and promotes success, iron will grind iron. If you and I remain in accountable relationships, we will eventually become sharp and shiny. Many times, we see accountability as a grind and making our life difficult.

Rough iron grinds, but the longer it suffers it becomes softer, smoother, and sharper. Be ready for grinding it out for a season, then get ready for the better you coming soon. It gets easier as you stay committed to the process and continually maintain the growth.

Ready, Aim...

In this season of life, what needs to be your target? Maybe you have two or three. These targets are areas you want improvement, putting an end to cycles of failure and defeat you've been repeating. Who are the men you can bring into your life to guard you and celebrate you? These don't just fall into place because you've read this chapter. Intentionality, not happenstance, determines the man you aspire to be. Right now, take some time to answer these questions.

Few men dare to take this step. If you make accountability your friend, you will be proud of the godly man you become. If you haven't already found mentors, grow some stones and do it.

COURAGE QUESTIONS

1. What's your response when it comes to mistakes you've made or failures you've had in the past? Do you blame, lie, try to find a way out, or just confess it?

2. What area in your life do you need to take more responsibility for your actions and institute accountability? How do you think it will infuse maturity?

3. Who are men in your life you believe care about you and want the best for you? Are you willing to invite them into your life, including the places you're not proud of, to help you grow as a man?

11

BRIDGE BURNER
FORGIVENESS

- The Absalom Struggle –

As he was sitting in his office addressing regular ministry tasks, Ryan was abruptly invited by another pastor to join him and the senior pastor in a meeting. This was a meeting in which Ryan sensed urgency, yet he had a relaxed and friendly relationship with the senior pastor and staff pastor. He casually walked in and sat down with both men, waiting to know what it was about and assuming there was a ministry issue he was unaware of. Surprisingly this would be the hardest and most agonizing meeting of his life.

As they waited for another person to join them, he was curious as to who else was coming to this important meeting. Unbeknownst to him, it would be his wife coming in to join them. She was also a little surprised herself and then the conversation began. It was in this meeting proof of his wife's infidelity was brought to light along with her confession. Ryan was overwhelmed with shock, grief, anger, pain, and became sick to his stomach. His world seemed to be crashing in as he learned of an intimate relationship his wife was having with another man. Although she initially denied it to escape the consequences of what she had done, she eventually admitted the truth.

The future months were filled with heartache and pain. Not only was their marriage destroyed, but they also had children experience a family being torn apart. The relationship was consumed by so much tension and pain she finally decided it was best to move out and allow Ryan to somehow figure out some normalcy for him and the kids. Ryan knew he needed to put his children's welfare first, but how do you care for them emotionally when you're suffering? As they proceeded throughout that year, he and the kids underwent professional counseling and assistance from other family members. As the wife was away, he grew more distant as he considered a divorce and continuing the separation. She, on the other hand, was beginning to realize the gravity of pain she caused by her actions. In Ryan's mind, the marriage was irreparable and so did she. Ryan had left his job and the community he was involved with as he was trying to move forward.

Over time something unpredictable began to happen. Ryan's heart was changing. As he strained to look through the eyes of his children, and yes, even the eyes of his wife, he began to have increasing compassion. Though he was resistant to try and rebuild their marriage and family, his heart was moving in a surprising direction. After months of personal counseling, he was willing to participate in counseling with his wife. The agony which came with the nightmare was still fresh, but he found himself open. Working on the thought to forgive was foreign to him for months, but it was becoming a consideration, and even a necessity. Forgiveness began to grow within him though it would take years, not months, for him and the marriage to recover.

Finally came the day when Ryan welcomed his wife home to carefully walk down the fragile road of restoration. It was arduous to say the least, but with God's tenderness they were able to move forward in healing. It's a lifelong commitment to enhance their marriage, and if you were to ask him how they were, he'd tell you the marriage is better than it ever was. It all began when he chose to humble himself and forgive the closest person to him who was undeserving due to her betrayal.

Ryan is a hero of mine. A man who is fearless and selfless in his pursuit to forgive.

RACIST IN THE MAKING

I met George in a group I started in the prison. He was locked up for life. He was convicted of multiple homicides and accepted the fact he'd never have a life on the outside. One murder he committed was filled with hate and racism. George was white, and his victim was a black man.

George grew up without his biological father in the picture. When he neared the age of seven, his mother married a man who became the stepfather to him and his sister. He was a large, intimidating black man with a volatile temper. George didn't understand why his new father figure wasn't fond of him. He somehow developed a disdain towards George and began giving cruel treatment to this second-grade boy. Eventually the new stepfather would sexually abuse him regularly and it lasted for years. Along with the abuse, the grown man would lock George in a bedroom for days, feeding him inconsistently, and provided a bucket for him to defecate in. Each week he would be allowed to visit the bathroom for a bath only to return to his room. To discourage George from escaping, the door was deadbolted and the bedroom window was covered with chicken wire. Though his mother and little sister knew of this treatment, they were both deathly afraid of the large man and fearful he would take George's life, as he threatened, if they ever told anyone. As time passed for months and grew into a couple years, the opportunity came for his sister to risk her life to save her brother and she helped him break free as they both ran away.

Of course, his stepfather would face the consequences for his horrific and beyond abusive treatment of this young boy when the authorities eventually got involved. George had experienced trauma he would carry for a lifetime. Unfortunately, it would come with an intense hate for black men and women. Sadly, they were what he naturally associated his pain and suffering with and had no plans to let go of. It's understandable he was filled with resentment and rage. How does one even encourage him to find forgiveness?

One day in his twenties he found himself in a violent conflict with a black man and, from the racism fueling his hard heart, he killed the man. This would lead to a conviction for the precious life he took. He confessed his guilt of murder and was sentenced to life. After finding

Christ in the institution, George was faced with the giant obstacle of forgiving the man who abused him for years. As he increasingly accepted the forgiveness of Christ, he found himself forgiving his then stepfather. As I sat with him in that group setting in prison he stated, surrounded by friendships with black and Hispanic inmates with whom he was loyal to, "if my stepfather walked in this room today, I would tell him I forgive him".

I'm in awe of this level of forgiveness, as I haven't personally ever experienced physical or sexual abuse, nor hate and racist attacks.

HIDDEN GRUDGES

For years I've proudly mentioned I don't hold grudges and I'm quick to forgive. I've always held the belief that unforgiveness just doesn't seem like a worthwhile way to live. As I was leading up to write this chapter, I disappointingly discovered that's not altogether true for me. I really want to be free from grudges but not too long ago an incident occurred, and it was hard for to forgive this time.

It came to my attention, and later confirmed, a man shared untrue things about me. It wasn't just to one individual but a few people, including some I admired and respected. I was deeply hurt by the man who slandered me, the words spoken, and naturally worried if those present would have a negative perception of me. My attempts to speak with him for understanding and reconciliation, as scripture outlines, were avoided. I finally arrived at the conclusion; the avoidance would require forgiveness on top of the forgiveness for the offense. I could live in frustration telling myself "this isn't fair", "this isn't right", "I'm gonna tell them", "they aren't getting away with this", etc. Or I could take the humble road to rise above and accept where the person is, let the problem rest, and prove otherwise to the hearers of the untrue statements. And if the offender ever grows to see their wrong, I'd be willing and free to talk about it.

Most things in life we can forgive but forgiveness isn't tested in the minor things. Unforgiveness seems to reveal itself when we're surprised by the unprepared injury received from another. The offenses of others can hurt our ego and pride which increases poor responses. World Champion Boxer Mike Tyson once said, "When I think I'm somebody, I get easily offended. When I think I'm nobody, I don't get offended." When you are an easily offended man, you're not bold and fearful, you're insecure and fragile.

As men I believe we struggle with forgiveness more than we think we do. We really have a problem moving forward when someone won't acknowledge their wrong or apologize. We decide to take the "tough guy" approach and shake it off, but it still can linger if left unaddressed in a healthy way. It's difficult to forgive when someone has embarrassed us, altered what others think about us, made us look weak, or has taken advantage of us. There are more circumstances I can list, but for us men, these examples can stir up some negative emotions and impact other areas.

According to a Johns Hopkins study, "Unforgiveness is linked to higher incidences of stress, heart disease, high blood pressure, lowered immune response, anxiety, depression, and other health issues. Broken relationships affect us deeply, especially when bitterness sets in. If someone you have an issue with is in the same room as you, you'll likely be tense, anxious, or angry the entire time, not doing your body or mind any favors. Forgiveness, on the other hand, is linked to a better overall sense of wellbeing."

How do you know if you haven't forgiven someone? The offense can be taking up "head space", you imagine having conversations to tell them off, you have angry thoughts about the person, you talk to a lot of people about the person and problem, or you plan to get justice for what has been done to you. Have you ever personally experienced any of these in operation? Frankly we begin to be consumed with how we've been treated.

THE LIFETIME OF A BURNED BRIDGE

Fortunately for us, there was a man in the Bible where we can learn how his unforgiveness, left unaddressed, led to his demise. Before we make the same mistake of unforgiveness, let's learn from Absalom's error and find out where we can get the power to forgive. He chose to burn bridges instead of rebuilding them.

King David had many sons, the best known was Solomon; among the others were Absalom, a warrior, and a beautiful sister named Tamar. On the other side of King David's vast land holdings was a half-brother named Amnon. Amnon saw Tamar and he was obsessed with her beauty, and, through deception, he tricks Tamar into entering his private tent and takes her by force and violates her. When it's over, he casts her out of his tent!

In that culture, no man would ever marry a woman that had been sexually abused or violated. Tamar would be doomed to a life of shame and loneliness. So, Tamar flees home; and her brother Absalom sees her distress and asks what happened? She tells Absalom what Amnon did, and Absalom is enraged. Their father David hears about this encounter and scripture says, "he was very angry", but disappointingly he never did anything. After two years of waiting, while unforgiveness and bitterness increased, Absalom decides to bring resolution to the matter.

Three steps transpired over the life of Absalom because he wouldn't forgive the offense of someone. These same steps can develop in us if we take the same posture as him.

Anger from the offense

> "...He hated Amnon deeply because of what he had done to his sister." (2 Samuel 13:21).

Absalom developed intense hostility towards Amnon as he nursed his anger over time. He was ruminating, meditating, and obsessively revisiting the wrongs done, over the offense and could not let it go. A bad attitude, disdain and a negative spirit will easily increase in our lives, only hurting ourselves. When anger is developing, it is our warning sign our behavior will be destructive if forgiveness is dismissed.

Bitterness towards the offender

> *"Absalom told his men, 'Wait until Amnon gets drunk; then at my signal, kill him'...So at Absalom's signal they murdered Amnon". (2 Samuel 13:28-29)*

After anger was steamrolling through the heart, mind, and soul of Absalom, bitterness was birthed in him. Bitterness creates a spirit within which reaps thoughts of settling the score, planning revenge, and not allowing someone to get away with what they have done. Are you wishing harm to the offender or even contributing to it? A bitter person is a hurt person, and hurt people will eventually hurt people.

Resentment towards offender's actions

> *"David then said to Abishai and all his officials, 'My son, who is of my own flesh, is trying to take my life.'" (2 Samuel 16:11).*

Prior to attempting to kill his father, Absalom made a lifestyle out of trying to destroy his dad. Whether it was stealing the hearts of people who loved his father David or destroying the property of David's army commander. From the time of Amnon's raping Tamar, Absalom grew in his anger, bitterness, and a life filled with resentment.

Absalom would end up losing his life trying to destroy David's army, along with the existence of compassion and forgiveness, as he was destined to murder his father. He lived believing hurting the offender would bring relief to his heart, but it never did. Unforgiveness killed Absalom.

The Boomerang

The author of this quote is unknown but is a sober perspective, *"Unforgiveness is like a boomerang; it comes back and hits you harder than the one who threw it."*

When we hold on to unforgiveness it's like keeping acid in our system and it will eventually kill us over time. We can't allow it to linger, or it will only create more damage in our lives. Look at how Absalom ruined his life by nurturing offense until the day he died. We may think withholding forgiveness is causing pain for the offender when it's really like drinking poison and waiting for the other person to die. Therefore, it is vital for godly men to be quick to forgive and not give the enemy room to destroy our hearts and minds.

Forgiveness is the decision or choice to give up the right for vengeance, retribution, and negative thoughts toward an offender to be free from anger and resentment. It requires a fearless man to look beyond the offense and look to God for strength to release the other person. You'll begin to discover what the work of forgiveness will accomplish in your spirit.

I WON'T FORGIVE HIM

Not only does withholding forgiveness hurt our relationships and plague our hearts, but it will also negatively affect our eternity and relationship with the Lord.

Keyshawn was disgusted by the betrayal of his business partner who was co-owner of the organization they founded together. His "friend" decided to leave the partnership, split the organization and take most of the clients they acquired together and left Keyshawn with few. I spoke with Keyshawn when the encounter was still fresh, he was furious and upset, and rightfully so. I tried to help him by being a listening ear and while also contributing ideas to navigate the recovery from the loss.

He was struggling to forgive, and I knew it would be a process, but the only way to move forward.

Each time I seen Keyshawn it would come up. It was more than upset. He had a desire to see the newly created business of his previous partner fall apart, and whenever he ran into a common friend he would make sure they knew how terrible he was. Unforgiveness had become and way of life which he was controlled by.

One day as we were talking, he made a very emphatic statement. He said with deep vengeance, "I will NEVER forgive him for what he did!" I was taken aback by where he had arrived because he had been a strong Christian man for years. Due to his maturity as a believer and the closeness of our relationship I decided to share something that was brutal to hear, but life giving at the same time. I knew he would understand and not argue.

I carefully shared, "Keyshawn if you won't forgive him, God will not forgive you. Not only will this deep heartache inflict pain on the rest of your life, but your eternity is also in jeopardy. You don't want that future." It was if he had never read Matthew 6:14-15, which my comments were referring to. The offense he received from a close person was ravaging his mental state, emotional state, spiritual state, and now, his relational place with God.

That day, in brokenness, Keyshawn made the hard decision to forgive and reject unforgiveness as a way of life. I was proud of his redirection and eventually witnessed him restoring that relationship. It wasn't easy and automatic, but consistent. As I shared in my first book, *"Forgiveness is not a one-time decision but a daily rehearsal."*

You and I will continually be in search of a peace we cannot find other than forgiving others. We will have tension within our hearts, tension with others (especially those who've wronged us), and tension with God. Romans 12:18 can be a guide with clear instruction, *"As far as it depends on you, live at peace with everyone"*, that leads us in living a life of forgiveness.

Forgiveness doesn't keep count, it loses count. In a world filled with offenses and addressing them in unhealthy ways, the church, godly men, must rise to be a light where our Savior shined the most…forgiveness.

COURAGE QUESTIONS

1. What offense have you had a hard time letting go of? Why haven't you released it?

2. When you think about forgiving an offense that was very painful, how does it make you feel?

3. If God will only forgive if we forgive others, how does that impact your urgency to forgive?

4. Who do you need to forgive at this moment? Are you willing to pray and commit to forgive that person? Why or why not?

12

SLAMMED SHUT
SUBMISSION

- The Cain Struggle –

I once met a man in his fifties who had been a Christian for a couple decades, and was a faithful church attender. As he reflected over coffee, somewhat disgruntled, he shared about "run-ins" he had over his life. Mainly he referred to his time in the Navy: he was a sailor in all senses of the term. During his term he was wild and crazy, while also obstinate and stubborn by his own admission. He had difficulties with superior officers constantly because he didn't like being ordered around and forced to do things when he really didn't want to. His behavior was documented on a more frequent basis, and he eventually wore out his welcome. He was discharged from the Navy due to his conduct. Unfortunately, his attitude and struggles have followed him throughout his life. When I had spoken on the topic of submission in a sermon he was irritated and bothered. Now he's a senior citizen and still wrestles with submitting to authority, especially when he doesn't like the person.

GRAPPLING WITH SUBMISSION

I want to warn you, in this chapter you might find yourself squirming and fidgeting as you read on. For some it's a foreign way of life that seems contrary to being a "real" man. Submission is one of man's greatest battles and a great asset at the same time. While obedience is focused on *what* we do, submission is revealed by *how* we do it. Why do I see this so important to address? I don't want you to miss the promise submission comes with.

Submission is unpopular inside and outside the church. Unbeknownst to the majority, God has carefully placed authority in our lives for us to discover a realm of blessings we are unaware of. In 1 Peter 2:18-19 (The Passion) we're told to, *"Submit to the authority…not only those who are kind and gentle but those who are hard and difficult. You find God's favor when you decide to please God even when you endure hardships…"* The promise we have in submitting to all authority is God's promotion and God's protection.

Unfortunately, men have negative responses to submission because of the culture we've been trained to think like. We believe that if I submit, I'm weak. I might be perceived as lower or less of a man. And sometimes we feel threatened we'll be taken advantage of. Instead of accepting who's in charge, we want to decide and approve who's in charge. Usually this means, if we hold to these ideals, we will push back against those who have authority in different environments we find ourselves in.

Submission to authority is an area I struggled with growing up as a young man who wanted to be respected. I innately wanted leaders in places of employment to do right by me or I would resist them. Or even worse I'd let them know how I felt. None of these responses were beneficial to me. It was in my mid-twenties I learned I was developing a rebellious spirit. I wanted to be honored and would dishonor anyone in charge of me when I chose to obey under my terms.

It was when I read scriptures like Romans 13:2 that my mentality was confronted, *"He who rebels against the authority is rebelling against what God has instituted."* As I learned more about rebellion and pride, I began to discover how submission was the way to freedom and blessing. Even though these truths were learned in my twenties, and have become strong convictions, I still see times when I lack a submissive spirit as a middle-aged man. It's a constant battle, but a battle I'm willing to fight.

CHIP ON YOUR SHOULDER

We often hear the phrase, "chip on your shoulder" in sports. It's perceived to be a positive trait for those who choose to be fierce competitors. The true source of this phrase gives a different picture than we have formed.

The origin of "chip on your shoulder" refers to a practice seen in America during the 19th century, in which boys looking for a fight would place an actual chip of wood on their shoulders before walking around belligerently daring others to knock the chip off. Could this be how we as men approach authority? As a generation who doesn't trust and/or defies authority, we're ready to protest and argue at the drop of a hat.

The chips on our shoulders we have are symbolic of pride. Droves of Christian men are missing the favor of God in their lives because they are plagued with a prideful spirit. A spirit which idolizes what they want and deserve, and even, yes, before God. Author Oswald Chambers, makes a strong statement in his book, "My Upmost for His Highest", *"Pride spits at the throne of God and says, 'I won't.'"* What an ugly picture of the behavior pride creates.

When pride is active within, it's not overtly obvious. I've noticed most times it's a shift in my attitude. Maybe you've seen pride show up as I have, in stubbornness. I can have a passive aggressive behavior displaying my disapproval or lack of cooperation. 1 Samuel 15:23 (NKJV) says, *"stubbornness is as iniquity and idolatry"*. Stubbornness reveals pride, we have put ourselves first, and dismiss submission to God and his will… and ultimately his favor on our lives.

HONOR AND HUMILITY

Tim and Cheryl made an appointment to meet with me in my office. They were both new in the church and had recently given their lives to Christ. It was so awesome to see their growth and passion. Tim and Cheryl wanted their lives and relationship to honor God in every area. As they learned more and more, they began to see areas in their lives that needed to be addressed. After we briefly chatted, Tim, in his blunt and direct personality, asked me, "where are we at?" He was referring to their relationship. They had been living together unmarried for a couple years and had children together. He wanted to know where they were in relation to sin in God's eyes and what they needed to do to "be right with God". Because he was a "give it to me straight" sort of guy I shared plainly they were living in sin by having sex outside of marriage. This also included living together since we are not to be associated with a "hint" of immorality. I explained they didn't have God's blessing on their relationship, but they could, and God wanted to bless it. I encouraged them to decide if they will marry or change living arrangements, and vow to live in sexual purity until a permanent decision was made. The next week they notified me they wanted to get married and asked me to marry them in my office as soon as they had the certificate. It was a wonderful moment to share.

Because Tim wanted to honor God and live under his hand of blessing, he was willing to submit to God, His Word, and the spiritual authority God placed in their lives. That's what godly men do.

They could have taken a posture of defiance and defense because I was judgmental or God was, or the Bible isn't relevant today. That would have a been a prideful response, but instead they wanted God's grace and touch on their lives.

James 4:6 (NIV) says, *"But he gives us more grace. That is why Scripture says: "God opposes the proud but gives grace to the humble."* We can be on the same side with God or choose to be his opponent determined to have our own way. In doing so we are guaranteed to lose out trying to get around God. We'll find ourselves fighting God or finding grace. We can't have both.

When you take on a spirit of humility and submission, you open up the door of God's favor in your life. Humility is, restraining my will and power by yielding to another, to my own benefit. I don't have to say the last word, be on top, demand respect, or always be right (in my mind at least). I choose to yield to the Lord, His Word, and the leaders he places in my life whether government, employment, or any other institution. All authority is of God, not all authority is godly. God even has a purpose for ungodly authority in our lives. This is no small task and only a secure and fearless man will choose to submit.

MASTER OR BE MASTERED

In the fourth chapter of Genesis, we see the conflict of Cain, firstborn son to Adam and Eve, and his battle with rebellion, pride, and submission. His attitude, anger, and jealousy proved to be his downfall as he rejected instruction from God.

> *"Abel kept flocks, and Cain worked the soil. In the course of time Cain brought some of the fruits of the soil as an offering to the LORD. But Abel brought fat portions from some of the firstborn of his flock. The LORD looked with favor on Abel and his offering, but on Cain and his offering he did not look with favor. So Cain was very angry, and his face was downcast. Then the LORD said to Cain, "Why are you angry? Why is your face downcast? If you do what is right, will you not be accepted? But if you do not do what is right, sin is crouching at your door; it desires to have you, but you must master it." Now Cain said to his brother Abel, "Let's go out to the field." And while they were in the field, Cain attacked his brother Abel and killed him. Then the LORD said to Cain, "Where is your brother Abel?" "I don't know," he replied. "Am I my brother's keeper?" The LORD said, "What have you done? Listen! Your brother's blood cries out to me from the ground. Now you are under a curse..." (vv. 2-11).*

So many men get swallowed up by their pride and end up in the same place, refusal to yield and submit to authority. When we follow similar steps of Cain, we are becoming rebellious. Rebellion creates hardness, bitterness, disobedience, division, and even provokes negative and ungodly behavior to take place. Which explains why 1 Samuel 15:23 (TLB) says, *"For rebellion is as bad as the sin of witchcraft"*. It's evil and wicked in the eyes of the Lord.

That's why we must remember the important perspective, submission to God's authority is your source of promotion and protection.

THE D'S OF REBELLION

Here are some typical attitudes and behaviors we have when a rebellious spirit is increasing within. Some are subtle, some blatant, but they can all serve as checkpoints for you when you're frustrated with the authority God has established over you.

Disagree with authority instead of honoring

> *"Cain and his offering he did not look with favor…Cain was very angry, and his face was downcast."*

I can understand disagreeing with God's decision. He had to bring from what Abel produced, instead of from his. We'd agree, that's not fair. There will be many things we disagree with in leaders and authority. Though we may disagree and become angry, it doesn't give us the right to voice it, complain, cause division, or protest. Honoring authority will always be to your benefit. Cain would prove his disagreement as the story unfolds.

Disqualify authority instead of respecting

> *"If you do what is right, will you not be accepted?"*

"That's not right!" is a common response. God promises everything will be fine but clearly Cain exalted his opinion above God's instructions, while doing what was right in his own eyes…nothing. Have you ever disapproved of authority's decisions, then disqualified them, believing they're wrong and my way is right? An attitude problem ensues and respect for authority is rejected. Of course, things will only get worse.

Discount authority instead of cooperating

> *"But if you do not do what is right, sin is crouching at your door"*

Here is the tipping point and decision to reject authority, do what is wrong, then sin begins filling our heart. It's funny because, usually at this stage we want to find evil, wrongdoings, and sin in the leader's life. We point out how they lie, cheat, don't respect us, and so on. Then we become the one succumbing our flesh and commit sin ourselves. When you find yourself not fully cooperating with authority, you are discounting their position.

Defy authority instead of serving

"You must master it."

We will either submit to God and his authority or submit to our flesh and sin. Which will you bow down to? Sin was crouching, Cain refused, and consequences followed his defiance. He served his bad attitude and decided he wouldn't serve at all. Instead of mastering the sin God warned him of, he was mastered. I've decided in times of these struggles to just shut up and serve. It will be my way through the hardship, without making things worse like Cain.

What do any of Cain's behaviors prove? Did Cain get him anywhere? He succumbed to weakness.

Opting for honor, respect, cooperation, and service aren't signs of weakness. Think of how many guys you know who aren't confident enough in who they are to pull this off. Only a fearless man will take these steps. It's almost impossible to hate a man or be malicious towards a man who is submissive.

SLAMMING THE DOOR ON REBELLION

When you're in a place of temptation to rebel against those in authority, ask yourself what God asked Cain, *"If you do what is right, will you not be accepted?"* The Devil is working overtime on you, wanting you to fail in weakness. He's leveraging false manhood and insecurity against you. When faced with refusal to yield, even slightly, to your flesh you will make things worse for yourself.

The answer in moments like these will always be to submit to God's authority instead of feeling manhood is threatened. Since our goal is submitting to authority God has put in place, this is a "you and God" issue. He's got us covered when we do, and every leader will answer to him. James 4:7 reassures us of victory through submission, *"Submit yourselves, then, to God. Resist the devil, and he will flee from you"*.

That's it. The fight is over. The strong man won.

?

COURAGE QUESTIONS

1. Do you believe submission to authority is a sign of strength? How?

2. Are you a submissive man? Why or why not?

3. How is submission to authority a good character trait for men?

4. In what conditions do you tend to refuse submission? What can do in the future to change?

13

RED FACED
ANGER

- The Moses Struggle –

I struggled deciding how much I would share about my own personal bouts with anger. As I am not proud of my sinful anger, because that's what it's been at times, I'm worried about what others think. I'm worried about what you, the reader, and others think about me in how I have dealt with anger in my past. I've asked myself why I'm shameful of sharing this area and the reason I come up with is it reveals the levels of self-control and immaturity. I don't know what your reasons may be for hiding the rages and fits you've thrown, but this was mine. I've come to the realization I'm not sharing as a confession to merely put myself on blast, but acknowledge where I've been, where I'm at, and where I'm headed when it comes to growing as a godly man. That's the context I share, with the hope you, the reader may be willing and open to assess your anger and where it may be hindering you.

WHOSE DAD IS THAT?

I was waiting in my car at the curb outside my daughter Leah's high school for the final school bell to ring so she could jump in the car for us to go home. My son and wife were with me, about 50 yards from the entrance, as we patiently waited for her. I had spoken to her several times about coming out to the car after briefly saying goodbye to her friends, so we didn't have to wait long. That day the bell had rung and, after five minutes of watching her talk to her friends, I was growing frustrated. It was almost ten minutes of tapping my fingers and fidgeting, expecting her to come to the car, as I knew she could see my car. Most kids were already out on the sidewalks walking home and the crowd was thinning. Finally, after "suffering" watching her slowly pace toward us caught in conversations and laughter, I had enough. I got out of my car and yelled (I'd rather say "raised my voice" as we Christians say in church, but it was yelling), "Leah get over here! We're all waiting for you, and I've told you before. Now let's go!" It wasn't only that I was shouting and embarrassing her, it was clear I was furious and red faced. My son pulled at me and tried to talk me down, but I snapped at him. Then my wife did, and well, I snapped at her too. My thought was, "Why are they mad at me when it's her fault?" At last, she got in the car upset and bitterness was on her face as I embarrassed her. Still, I had a few more words to share. It was a terrible moment for me as a dad, husband, and, oh yeah, a pastor too.

That day is so clear in my mind as I recall the situation and it still stings. I was in my forties throwing a pitiful tantrum. After my anger subsided over the next hour or so, I was filled with remorse and shame. I began to examine what I had done to my daughter, and knew I let my family down in portraying myself as a fool. I had to make amends with my daughter by asking for forgiveness. I also apologized to my wife and son. It was after that I realized; I've got to do something about my anger. I was not proud, and deeply ashamed of how I behaved that day. I didn't want to admit it was out of control, but let's just say it was occasionally controlling me. That's not the type of man I want to be.

This scripture inflicts a sting on me in Proverbs 29:11 (AMP), *"A fool always loses his temper and displays his anger, but a wise man [uses self-control] and holds it back."* I don't want to live foolishly losing my temper and creating that reputation for myself, in and out of my home.

OUTRAGE-OUS AT HOME

Gary's wife came to our church office seeking to speak with me for direction as she was at the end of her rope, always acquiescing to his fury and concerned about the effects of it on their son. His job came with stress and the demands for working extra hours. Since he was the one working a full-time job, he had expectations of the manner in which his home should function.

In Gary's mind, he had the job with more stress and long hours, so his preferences ruled the home. He expected his wife to have dinner waiting after she had cleaned the house. It was "her job" to shop for groceries, do the laundry, take out the trash, while she also kept an eye on their young boy. When things might be a little messy or dinner wasn't prepared, he would throw a fit. She would try to explain but he would only grow angrier. Then she would get upset and shouting matches ensued. He went to another level as he would call her ugly names, degrade her, and condemn her for being a terrible wife. Exploding into rages became regular in their home, as his son observed how Gary treated his mother and responded to tension.

Gary could not let go of his perspective that he worked hard for his home to be perfect therefore his family should accommodate his justified, volatile outbursts.

It's usually when we can't get control of our emotions, and subject them to patience, we lose our cool. In different versions of the Bible, patience is also referred to as long suffering. The question for each of us is, how long can we suffer and still manage our frustrations and irritation? If we have a "quick fuse" or can't control anger in a healthy way, it will attract sinful behavior. Anger appears to be the biggest struggle for most men. They just don't know how to release anger in a healthy way, or have processes in which they keep from sin.

In Ephesians 4:26 explains, *"Be angry, and do not sin"*. So, when has anger become sin? For many, separating anger and sin is difficult to identify. Some can't see getting angry while not carrying on in sinful ways and I've met some men who don't think anger is ok. Where's the line?

Further on in Ephesians chapter four, verse 31 outlines other sin that comes along with unbridled anger. It tells us to, *"Let all bitterness and indignation and wrath (passion, rage, bad temper) and resentment (anger, animosity) and quarreling (brawling, clamor, contention) and slander (evil-speaking, abusive or blasphemous language) be banished from you, with all malice (spite, ill will, or baseness of any kind)."* That's a pretty hefty list. Other poor behaviors can be putting a hole through the wall, going to porn, walking out on the family, heavy drinking, or sadly for some, putting their hands on people.

There will always be a cost for lack of self-control when we're angry. Respect and reputation can dwindle or disappear altogether when we give in to our temper. We can also ruin opportunities because we have lost credibility or trust from those who believe in us. What contributes to build up anger inside of us and damaging ourselves is due to the pressure we take on as men. We may have societal expectations, pressure, stress, relationship conflicts, and unresolved trauma we haven't seen as landmines, and we're stomping all over them.

BETWEEN A ROCK AND A MAD PLACE

We see in a Moses, a man who was just like us, have anger issues which showed up on difficult or challenging occasions. When he was younger, he actually took someone's life in a heated altercation leading him to leave Egypt. Some of the times righteous anger was justified, but how he handled it proved to be an Achille's Heel for him. His anger would eventually get the best of him, and his life mission, and cost him dearly.

We discover in Numbers 20, a moment when Moses appears to be suffering for too long with his emotions and begins losing his battle to control his anger. The children of Israel God has made him the leader of, are upset with Moses. This is usually the case if you are in a leadership role and you're not providing people with what they need or want. They will begin to talk and even play dirty at times.

The three million plus, people group Moses was leading began turning on him. They had moments of trial along their long journey and would begin to make Moses the target of their frustrations and anger. In this account they have no water to drink, the people are questioning Moses, and talking about how things used to be better and not as bad in Egypt. This was hurting him so he did the right thing – he took it all to the Lord. Take note of the most important thing we can do is follow the model Moses provides. But after he finished his time with the Lord and had received instructions, he returned to his unresolved anger. Here is what transpired:

> *"Moses and Aaron went from the assembly to the entrance to the Tent of Meeting and fell facedown, and the glory of the Lord appeared to them. The Lord said to Moses, "Take the staff, and you and your brother Aaron gather the assembly together. Speak to that rock before their eyes and it will pour out its water. You will bring water out of the rock for the community so they and their livestock can drink." So Moses took the staff from the Lord's presence, just as he commanded him. He and Aaron gathered the assembly together in front of the rock and Moses said to them, "Listen, you rebels, must we bring you water out of this rock?" Then Moses raised his arm and struck the rock twice with his staff. Water gushed out, and the community and their livestock drank. But the Lord said to Moses and Aaron, "Because you did not trust in me enough to honor me as holy in the sight of the Israelites, you will not bring this community into the land I give them.""*

Moses decides to take matters into his own hands, abort God's instructions, and scold these people who have hurt and attacked him. Instead of giving honor to the Lord, and building the faith of the people, he decides to forego speaking to the rock and slamming the staff twice on the rock. He railroaded God and took power he didn't have. If I was God, I would've turned the water off and let Moses look like a fool when he struck the rock, but that's me. God allows it to go on and let Moses behave as he wanted and knew was wrong.

What was devastating in the outcome for Moses giving full vent to his anger. The journey he had led the people on for decades to enter the promise land would not include him in the final stages. God judged him for his outburst and rage, and all those who were alive would enjoy the land "flowing with milk and honey" while he was only allowed to see it from a distance.

Anger cost Moses in a big way, and it will be the same for us if we don't decide to take control of it.

SHIFTING GEARS

When we're good and angry we usually push the petal to the metal with roaring and for many, obscenities. Then you find yourself caught in shouting matches with others without even hearing them, their reasons, or what they have to say. We take off and there's no turning back. Hours later, or the next morning we wake up, we come to our senses and realized what a fool we've been.

In the book of James, we're given new insight to help us process our anger for better outcomes. What we read seems so backwards and not a rational way to handle it. It may be that we're so conformed to toxic anger we can't see how you can ever see something good come out of a situation that has caused anger to arise. In chapter one verse 19 it says, *"Understand this, my dear brothers and sisters: You must all be quick to listen, slow to speak, and slow to get angry."* You may have never considered this way before, and you're stuck thinking it will never work and you're too mad to just listen someone else ramble.

Hear James and the spirit of his words. The quicker you are to hear the other person for understanding, and more careful to talk without shouting, will delay your anger. Don't wait until you have reached your boiling point to try and have control, reach for control when you feel you're getting warm on the inside. You can slow your anger if you're willing to hear the other person out and carefully proceed for a reasonable outcome, which doesn't necessarily mean it's your way.

As godly men, I believe it's up to us to determine the emotional climate in a situation. It's important we become leaders and direct others involved to a pleasing resolve. When we take this perspective, we begin to see the need to control our anger by what we say and how we respond.

GO AHEAD

Our family loves to go on vacation in southern California and spend several days at the beaches. My favorite beach town is Huntington Beach. I enjoy the shops on Main Street, the restaurants, and the overall vibe.

After dinner one night our family decided to take a stroll around the area as sundown neared. When the sun goes down in that nucleus of blocks things can get crazy as crowds gather at the clubs and some begin to lose control of their sobriety. We were headed to our car, sidestepping a crowd on the sidewalk and I could see a group of guys approaching so I moved to get out of their way for them to continue on. One guy, in his early twenties, was walking through the separation of our family and decided to put his arm around my 13-year-old daughter's waist and with 90 proof breath said, "Hey baby". That was it! He inappropriately touched my daughter and I refused to let that be something to shrug off as protector of my family. I turned around and lunged to grab him. I wanted to snatch him by the shirt and throw him up against the wall and make it clear to him and everyone, I defend my family and I will even fight for them. Before doing so, I reached through the small crowd as bouncers from the club rushed to stop me along with other guys. I wouldn't be fully honest if I left out how I was pushing them out of the way too. One friend of the foolish young man shouted, "Sorry man, he's drunk". My thought was, then it'll be easier to knock him out. Just kidding, sort of.

On the sidewalk that night fury and anger came over me to protect and defend my family, without apologizing. It wasn't a reckless out of control rage, it was standing for what's right while remaining godly. I didn't use foul language, behave mean-spirited, or anything else. Why do I share this story? Because some people have a perception Christian men can't show anger, which this is false. Being a Christian doesn't mean men become wimps, carpets for people to walk on, and act like things are ok when they're seriously wrong. This may not be popular with some, but we have been given testosterone and masculinity from God for a reason. A secure and confident, godly man knows when, how, and why to turn the anger switch on and use it for good. It's immature to be full of wrath, vengeful, mean, a hothead, or explode into a rage because something or someone inconvenienced you. That's self-centeredness and emotionally out of control. Anger is a God-given emotion to be used in a healthy way for just causes, protection, and defending others. I will be indignant with a righteous anger for the defenseless, the poor, the hurting, people treated unjustly, and my family. You're the man, the leader of your home so utilize this emotion when necessary. My daughter, and son, needed to see their dad stand up for her, to protect her and to defend her. Hopefully she marries a man who will be just like her dad in this area, as well as my son with those he cares for.

Go ahead, be angry. You have God's permission to, unapologetically, if you maintain self-control.

PULL OVER GENTLY

I was travelling to a location in my car and had another man follow me in his car on the way there so we could discuss a project we would be working on together. In California, homelessness was at an all-time high throughout the city where we lived. Many of the homeless people living in tarps and boxes, and out of shopping carts were either on drugs or possessed a mental illness.

As I pulled into the parking lot, I noticed a homeless man straggling around, talking into the sky and with a scowl on his face. After I parked, the other man I was with pulled in and he drew closer to the homeless man. Then that man walking gave a middle finger to the man driving. This sparked an angry reaction as he yelled at the homeless man, before swerving hard into a parking space and jumping out of his truck. I could tell he was ready to get in the homeless man's face and things could've gotten way out of hand. I was stunned he would allow a man in that mental state to get him fired up. I jumped in front of him before he proceeded and asked him, "What are you doing? Are you really going to jump on a man who doesn't know where he's going, or what he's saying or even gesturing?" I ended up helping him relax and give thought to where he was at personally when it came to rage, wrath, and anger. He was a much better man than the behavior he displayed in that parking lot.

It's amazing how words can impact our anger. Our tone can soothe our wrath and the wrath of another person as well. Proverbs 15:1 empowers us by stating, *"A gentle answer deflects anger, but harsh words make tempers flare."* If you take the avenue to speak carefully, softer, without being harsh, you'll experience the power you have, to minimize the heat of anger.

You have the power to master your anger. Godly men refuse to be controlled by their unbridled anger.

COURAGE QUESTIONS

1. Is or is not, controlling your anger a struggle for you? Explain.

2. What can cause you to lose your temper? Why?

3. How can you make corrections in weak moments of anger to have a healthier outcome?

THE ULTIMATE FEARLESS MAN

Throughout the previous chapters we have covered accounts of men in the Bible, identifying with their struggles, deficiencies, and self-sabotage. I've shared true life stories of men who faced pain and disappointments, helping us reduce our self-condemnation, defeat, and shame within. Now we make a shift to stop living like common men and start living like Christ.

Until this point, I have withheld accounts of Jesus demonstrating high and fearless levels of living. Comparing ourselves to Jesus' strong example, who was without failures or flaws, can cause us to excuse ourselves from living like Jesus become it seems out of reach. But what we can learn from Christ is that he was not excused from facing struggles and temptations us men face. Because Jesus was the ultimate and victorious fearless man, he is our measuring stick and inspiration. Jesus had hard and difficult decisions to make to avoid self-sabotaging his own life and purpose. Not only did he make these courageous decisions, but he also passed them on to us so that we can choose to be godly and fearless men, committed to follow him. There is no wiggle room when Jesus draws line after line challenging our commitment to him.

In John 6:66-67 (BSV), after a tough and brutal speech filled with truth, Jesus communicates the cost a follower of Christ must pay. The scripture reads, *"From that time on, many of his disciples turned back and no longer walked with him. So, Jesus said to the Twelve, 'Do You want to leave too?'"*

This is an "all or nothing" lifestyle we're invited to join. Jesus is giving an ultimatum, are you in or out? It's your choice but pick one. Will you follow or withdraw, choose godliness or worldliness, have biblical manhood or cultural manhood, be a casual Christian or a faithful Christian? Does this seem extreme? Yes, it is. And Jesus has no problem communicating it. How will you choose to live?

Fearless men dare to, and decide to, give up their lives while wimpy men shrink back. Jesus doesn't suggest, but requires a man to give up his financial, spiritual, sexual, relational, and career lives. If He's not Lord of all, He's not Lord at all, and there is no compartmentalizing these areas. We offer every area in exchange for a full, wide open, healed, favored, and confident life! Are you willing to be courageous and let go of the familiar? Only a man opting for a godly life will respond with yes.

The test of a fearless man is how a man handles pressure, resistance, and adversity. You can live trying to manage your struggles and self-sabotage, or you can live with courage to overcome them. As we look at the life of Jesus, we find ways to confront challenges head on like he did. The goal isn't to come out strong and tough, or trying to prove ourselves. He didn't focus on impressing others or proving himself. He just lived with godly masculinity. Friend, you don't have to prove anything to anyone if you live with godly masculinity. That's where we discover freedom in Christ.

IMAGINE THIS...

Can you imagine how Jesus would have appeared if he chose to be a common man instead of the ultimate fearless man? He would have striven to appear tough when he needed help and was vulnerable to failure. He could've chosen to take sexual advantage of ladies who loved and followed him. Maybe he would've lost control, fought back, and hunted down people who betrayed and plotted to kill him. To feel valued, he might have tried to impress others, desperately wanting to be liked. Or he could have pursued success and importance, by accumulating toys and a big house, while abandoning God's will for his life. He might have chosen to prove his manhood by never crying in front of people. Maybe he would get revenge on people who were spreading rumors, trying to prove him a fraud, or spit on him. It would have been terrible to read he chose to write Peter off for denying him. Jesus probably would have secrets and behaviors on the side nobody knew about. He might disobey or not submit to God and leaders because he was too insecure and would appear weak. He would have made excuses for giving into temptation or blame someone else for it. After performing miracles, he'd stand up and gloat, becoming arrogant and demanding respect. He wouldn't have washed the disciple's feet; they would've surely taken turns to wash his. He might have run from the cross because it wasn't fair, people stopped supporting him, and wouldn't give him his "flowers".

What a sad definition of who Jesus could have been. This is what a fearful, insecure, and broken man looks like. But he was nothing of the sort we read about in the scriptures. The more I focus on the controlled humanity and character of Jesus, I'm moved just as much as the miracles and love he demonstrated. It actually empowers me to become like Christ.

THE C'S OF CHRIST

As we move forward living as Fearless Men, let's look at how Jesus defeated the struggles common men have wrestled with for thousands of years. The "C's" of Christ give focus to follow his extreme footsteps in adversity, fear, or weakness.

Closeness

> "He took Peter and Zebedee's two sons, James and John, and he became anguished and distressed. He told them, "My soul is crushed with grief to the point of death. Stay here and keep watch with me." (Matthew 26:37-38, NLT).

Jesus was vulnerable in his time of weakness and poured his heartbreak out with no shame. Develop closeness with godly men, whom you can be fully honest for mutual support, encouragement, and a place of refuge. Jesus displays his need of friends and didn't try to face life alone. Trying to prove you're a tough guy or thinking you can handle it will lead you to a dead end.

Confidence

> *"The Father and I are one." Once again, the people picked up stones to kill him. Jesus said, "At my Father's direction I have done many good works…" (John 10:30-31, NLT).*

Jesus' had confidence over insecurities because he knew who he was in the Father, not in how he appeared to people. Your self-esteem must be built on what God says, so you don't spend life trying to meet other's expectations.

Constant

> *"The Lord turned and looked straight at Peter. Then Peter remembered the word the Lord had spoken to him: 'Before the rooster crows today, you will disown me three times.'" (Luke 22:61).*

Though Jesus was abandoned and betrayed by his friends, he didn't quit on his destiny. He was resilient and went on to endure abuse and crucifixion. No matter what comes your way or if you have past regrets, don't give up. Don't allow your failures, brokenness, or struggles have the final say in your life. Never give up.

Commissioned

> *"The Son of Man came to seek out and to give life to those who are lost." (Luke 19:10, TPT).*

Jesus' identity was found in the mission God put in him. God has given each of us a unique identity to accomplish his plan through us. Live in your divine purpose, passion, and identity without bending. Don't allow labels from men kill the man God created you to be.

Comfortable

> *"Jesus told him, 'Foxes have holes, and birds have nests, but the Son of Man has nowhere to sleep.'" (Matthew 8:20, GW).*

Jesus, as the Messiah, wasn't entitled nor did he search for satisfaction in earthly treasures and pleasures. He was content and comfortable with much or little. Supersizing your life with possessions won't make you comfortable within.

Conviction

"Even though Jesus was God's Son, he learned obedience from the things he suffered. In this way, God qualified him..." (Hebrews 5:8-9, NLT).

It was in the hard things Jesus proved his obedience to fulfill the Father's will. Obey God in every detail, every day, and you will discover God's will for your life. God rewarded Jesus for his lifelong obedience. With conviction to obey God completely, without compromising, will not result in a wasted life.

Completeness

"And a voice from heaven said, 'This is my Son, whom I love, and I am very pleased with him.'" (Matthew 3:17, NCV).

Before Jesus performed a miracle, taught a class, or even hung on the cross, he was a success. His life was not complete and full because of what he did, but who he was in the eyes of God first. Don't squander life trying to have success, your worth isn't found in what you accomplish. Who you are is more important than what you do.

Consistent

"They came to him and said, 'Teacher, we know you are a man of integrity. You aren't swayed by men, because you pay no attention to who they are'..." (Mark 12:14).

What a statement of a consistent life! Jesus was the same man in every season, occasion, and with all people. Dependability and integrity are demonstrated by our daily decisions to honor God, especially when no one is looking.

Consecrated

> *"This High Priest of ours understands our weaknesses, for he faced all of the same testings we do, yet he did not sin." (Hebrews 4:15, NLT).*

Yes, he was even tempted with sexual immorality. It reads, "all the same testings". The High Priest separated himself for holiness in the eyes of God. Keep your temple, your entire being, holy recognizing your sexuality doesn't belong to you.

Committed

> *"Jesus took Peter and the brothers, James and John, and led them up a high mountain. His appearance changed from the inside out, right before their eyes…" (Matthew 17:1-2, MSG).*

Jesus was committed to his small, selected group of confidants. It was before their eyes that he was transformed. If you want to continually transform in Christ, commit to bring brothers into your life who will challenge and celebrate you as you progress in faith and life.

Covering

> *"Jesus said, "Father, forgive them, for they do not know what they are doing." (Luke 23:34).*

In the final moments of living 33 years on earth, Jesus looked over all the moments of mankind's ugliness and spoke forgiveness with grace and love. Even when others know what they're doing to us, or do it on purpose, it's to your emotional and eternal benefit to cover what others do in forgiveness instead of carrying offenses through life.

Compliant

> *"But he gave up his place with God and made himself nothing… and became like a servant…he humbled himself and was fully obedient to God, even when that caused his death—death on a cross." (Philippians 2:7-8, NCV).*

Whether it was before God only, or those with earthly authority, Jesus submitted as a servant without any rights. We're going to be ordered to do things, along with mistreatment sometimes. When your pride is increasing, remind yourself you're only a servant like Christ and you'll find freedom living in compliance.

Composure

> *"He did not retaliate when he was insulted, nor threaten revenge when he suffered. He left his case in the hands of God, who always judges fairly." (1 Peter 2:23, NLT).*

Jesus had plenty of reasons to go into a rage, lash out, get revenge, fight back and so forth. But he decided to keep godly composure and allow the Father to have the final say, and we admire him for his strength. If you choose to lose control of your anger, and dismiss composure, it will be to the detriment of relationships with others…and your Heavenly Father.

A FEARLESS FUTURE

Following Christ is not flimsy commitment many churches allow. We create soft, powerless, religious men instead of godly men when we lower the bar. The great evangelist Billy Graham once said, "Salvation is free, but discipleship will cost you your life." Stop settling and making excuses for shallow, convenient, and weak Christianity. God doesn't expect you to be perfect, only persistent. Make Jesus' plan of attack the same for you. Be a man, a godly and fearless man…like Him.

Remember what Jesus said to his friends, *"Do You want to leave too?"* What will your response be to future weaknesses, insecurities, struggles, and failures?

Dare to be a fearless follower of Christ…without flinching.

"FEAR NOT"

— Jesus.

ABOUT THE AUTHOR

DAVE NOVAK
MINISTRIES

Dave Novak is a former, founding lead pastor in Sacramento, California for over 15 years. His ministry has been shaped in racially diverse cultures and non-churched contexts, giving him a relevant voice of hope. He is the author of "No More Dad Issues", a book of healing and freedom. In July of 2023, Dave founded The F2 Project focused on healing dad issues and helping dads become heroes. He is a sought-after speaker and ordained with the Assemblies of God. Dave and Lori married in 1999 and have two adult children, Leah and Titus.

To book Dave for events visit: www.davenovakministries.com

Instagram: @TheDaveNovak

THE F2 PROJECT

FATHERS 2 FATHERLESS

In July of 2023, Dave founded a non-profit ministry called, The F2 Project. The mission of this movement is to heal dad issues and help dads to become heroes. Dave is taking this ministry into different churches, cities, and prisons with groups and courses.

To learn more about powerful ministry visit: www.thef2project.com

Instagram: @thef2project

MORE FROM DAVE

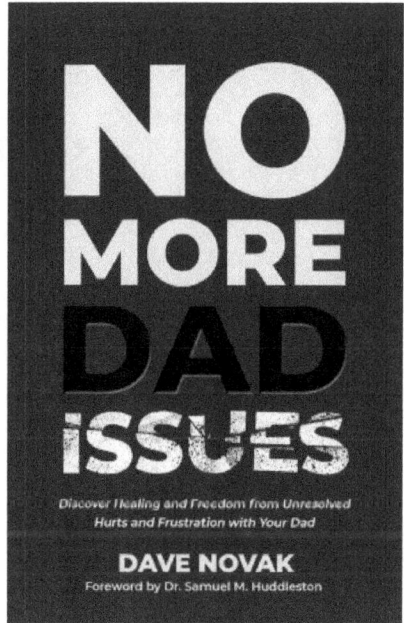

Purchase anywhere books are sold.

END NOTES

CHAPTER 1

#1
James Madison University
"Counseling Center: Vulnerability"
https://www.jmu.edu/counselingctr/self-help/relationships/vulnerability.shtml

#2
Dr. Brene Brown *"Daring Greatly"* (2015)

CHAPTER 3

Formula 409
https://www.formula409.com/about-us

CHAPTER 5

Christin Ditchfield, *"Deion Sanders: Chasing the Wind"*
Viet Christian
https://vietchristian.com/gospel/DeionSanders.asp

Psychologist Erich Fromm
Forbes Quotes: Thoughts on the Business Life
https://www.forbes.com/quotes/2756/

CHAPTER 6

Dr. John Maxwell, *"Spiritual Reproduction"*
https://www.sermoncentral.com/content/a-John_Maxwell_07_23_07

CHAPTER 7

Harvard Business Review, *"How High Achievers Overcome Their Anxiety"*
https://hbr.org/webinar/2023/03/how-high-achievers-overcome-their-anxiety#:~:text=Complimentary%20HBR%20Webinar,-Tuesday%2C%20April%2011&text=00%20pm%20ET-,Here's%20a%20secret%3A%20A%20

surprising%20number%20of%20extremely%20successful%20people,what%20
psychologists%20call%20thought%20traps.

CHAPTER 8

Tim Mak, Politico, "9 Best Alan Simpson Quotes"
https://www.politico.com/story/2012/05/9-best-alan-simpson-quotes-076711

CHAPTER 9

The Cleveland Clinic, *"Sex Addiction, Hypersexuality, and Compulsive Sexual Behavior"*
https://my.clevelandclinic.org/health/diseases/22690-sex-addiction-
hypersexuality-and-compulsive-sexual-behavior#:~:text=Sex%20addiction%20
refers%20to%20excessive,sexual%20behavior%20and%20other%20names.

CHAPTER 10

Professor Robert Anthony, Harvard Business School
"Terry Barber: A successful business owner gets rid of blame and distrust"
https://www.craigdailypress.com/news/terry-barber-a-successful-business-
owner-gets-rid-of-blame-and-distrust/

CHAPTER 11

John's Hopkins Medicine
Seattle Christian Counseling, *"The Dark Side of Unforgiveness"*
https://seattlechristiancounseling.com/articles/the-dark-side-of-unforgiveness

CHAPTER 12

Oswald Chambers, "My Utmost for His Highest"
"Continuous Conversion"